W9-BCK-260

Raw, Quick & Delicious!

5-ingredient recipes in just 15 minutes

Douglas McNish

Robert
ROSE

Raw, Quick & Delicious!

Text copyright © 2013 Douglas McNish

Recipe photographs copyright © 2013 Robert Rose Inc.

Cover and text design copyright © 2013 Robert Rose Inc.

No part of this publication may be reproduced, stored in a retrieval system or transmitted, in any form or by any means, without the prior written consent of the publisher or a licence from the Canadian Copyright Licensing Agency (Access Copyright). For an Access Copyright licence, visit www.accesscopyright.ca or call toll-free: 1-800-893-5777.

For complete cataloguing information, see page 221.

Disclaimer

The recipes in this book have been carefully tested by our kitchen and our tasters. To the best of our knowledge, they are safe and nutritious for ordinary use and users. For those people with food or other allergies, or who have special food requirements or health issues, please read the suggested contents of each recipe carefully and determine whether or not they may create a problem for you. All recipes are used at the risk of the consumer.

We cannot be responsible for any hazards, loss or damage that may occur as a result of any recipe use.

For those with special needs, allergies, requirements or health problems, in the event of any doubt, please contact your medical adviser prior to the use of any recipe.

Design and Production: Kevin Cockburn/PageWave Graphics Inc.

Editor: Judith Finlayson

Recipe Editor: Tracy Bordian

Copy Editor: Gillian Watts

Proofreaders: Gillian Watts/Tracy Bordian

Indexer: Gillian Watts

Nutritional Consultant: Doug Cook, RD, MHSc

Recipe Photography: Colin Erricson

Associate Photographer: Matt Johannsson

Food Styling: Kathryn Robertson

Prop Styling: Charlene Erricson

Other photographs: Mosaic Page #1: Celery © istockphoto.com/fcafotodigital; Cumin Seeds © istockphoto.com/wragg; Red Onions © istockphoto.com/FotografiaBasica; Turmeric Powder © istockphoto.com/zkruger; Button Mushrooms © istockphoto.com/tbradford; Fresh Strawberries © istockphoto.com/Rinelle; Mint © istockphoto.com/magdasmith; Red Peppers © istockphoto.com/xavierarnau; Walnuts © istockphoto.com/FotografiaBasica; Mosaic Page #2: Basil Leaves © istockphoto.com/bluestocking; Acorn Squash © istockphoto.com/Stieglitz; Watermelons © istockphoto.com/THEPALMER; Curry Powder © istockphoto.com/alejandrophotography; Fresh Blueberries © istockphoto.com/Kativ; Carrots © istockphoto.com/DOUGBERR; White Cauliflower © istockphoto.com/Infografick; Sugar Snap Peas © istockphoto.com/bedo; Pumpkin Seeds © istockphoto.com/Lcc54613; Mosaic Page #3: Pistachios © istockphoto.com/101cats; Vineyard Grapes © istockphoto.com/kcline; Oregano © istockphoto.com/TheRachelKay; Grapefruit © istockphoto.com/KirbusEdvard; Olive Oil © istockphoto.com/surely; Cinnamon © istockphoto.com/MKucova; Key Limes © istockphoto.com/susabell; Sweet Potatoes © istockphoto.com/Jonathan Austin Daniels; Pineapple © istockphoto.com/YinYang; Mosaic Page #4: Pecan Halves © istockphoto.com/1MoreCreative; Dill Leaves © istockphoto.com/Nomadsoul1; Coconut © istockphoto.com/olgakr; Oranges © istockphoto.com/Dimitris66; Eggplant © istockphoto.com/THEPALMER; Nutmeg © istockphoto.com/wragg; Green Kale © istockphoto.com/THEPALMER; Tomatoes © istockphoto.com/JoeBiafore; Bean Sprouts © istockphoto.com/stuartbur; Mosaic Page #5: Beets © istockphoto.com/ROTTSTRA; Almonds © istockphoto.com/FotografiaBasica; Bananas © istockphoto.com/miskolin; Agave Nectar © istockphoto.com/sf_foodphoto; Avocados © istockphoto.com/PhilLedwith; Portobello & Crimini Mushrooms © istockphoto.com/kcline; Cucumbers © istockphoto.com/xxmmxx; Raspberries © istockphoto.com/molka; Cilantro © istockphoto.com/massman; Mosaic Page #6: Cashews © istockphoto.com/Suzifoo; Yellow and Green Zucchini © istockphoto.com/Sarsmis; Apples © istockphoto.com/JoeBiafore; Lemons © istockphoto.com/StephanHoerold; Paprika © istockphoto.com/stachelpferdchen; Parsley © istockphoto.com/MmeEmil; Pears © istockphoto.com/SensorSpot; Baby Spinach © istockphoto.com/Kativ; Sunflower Seeds © istockphoto.com/FotografiaBasica;

Cover image: Carrot Pad Thai (page 150)

We acknowledge the financial support of the Government of Canada through the Book Publishing Industry Development Program (BPIDP) for our publishing activities.

Published by Robert Rose Inc.

120 Eglinton Avenue East, Suite 800, Toronto, Ontario, Canada M4P 1E2

Tel: (416) 322-6552 Fax: (416) 322-6936

www.robertrose.ca

Printed and bound in Canada

1 2 3 4 5 6 7 8 9 MP 21 20 19 18 17 16 15 14 13

Raw, Quick & Delicious!

GLEN COVE PUBLIC LIBRARY
4 GLEN COVE AVENUE
GLEN COVE, NEW YORK 11542-2885

Contents

Acknowledgments

First and foremost I want to thank my mother and father for encouraging me to read and write at an early age. Without them I would not be able to do what I do or be the person I am today.

To my amazing wife, Candice, for showing me what unconditional love truly is, being the best friend I could ever ask for and teaching me the mantra "Find Peace and Contentment in Everything You Do."

To Lisa, Rob, Joey, Ryan and Andy for being my home away from home. I may not always make Andy happy, but no one can touch my sushi!

To Bob Dees for his business savvy and pursuit of excellence.

To Judith Finlayson for her constant support and guidance from day one.

To my amazing editor Tracy Bordian for her sense of humor and relentless attention to detail. Maybe next time we can dance more quickly and that snow will actually go away!

Thanks to the group at PageWave Graphics, especially designer Kevin Cockburn. Also to photographer Colin Erricson, associate photographer Matt Johannsson, prop stylist Charlene Erricson and food stylist Kathryn Robertson. And to copy editor Gillian Watts.

For all those who live, or have ever sought to live, a healthy, compassionate and active lifestyle, this book is for you.

Introduction

I have spent the better part of the past few years talking about the benefits of a raw vegan diet at events throughout North America. After explaining why people would want to abandon pots of bubbling chili or crispy potatoes in exchange for kale salads and coconut cream tarts, I inevitably get the same questions: "Doesn't raw food take a long time to prepare?" "Isn't it complicated to make, requiring a lot of special kitchen equipment?" The answer to both is a resounding no. Raw food can be as simple to make as Lime, Tomato and Avocado Chili (page 161), Sweet Potato Enchilada (page 160) and Pineapple Coconut Crumble (page 204) — all can be prepared in 15 minutes or less.

Sure, many raw recipes require equipment such as a high-powered blender or a dehydrator. And some dishes demand that you sprout grains, which is time-consuming. While those recipes definitely have a place in raw cuisine, many others rely on the simple preparation of fresh fruits and vegetables to create satisfying dishes in a matter of minutes. By using the right techniques and only five ingredients, the recipes in this book showcase how quickly and effortlessly raw food can be prepared, often even more so than traditional cuisine.

When I create raw recipes, I manipulate the shape, texture or flavor of foods in ways that make them reminiscent of traditional cuisine, with the goal of creating meals that are as pleasing to the palate. In this book you won't find recipes that require hours of soaking, sprouting or dehydrating. Instead you will find dishes that rely on fresh fruits and vegetables marinated in citrus juice and cold-pressed olive oil and finished with nutritious nuts and seeds. Anyone, regardless of skill level or experience, can make these recipes using standard kitchen equipment.

Sometimes you may want to enhance the flavors of a recipe or keep a "go to" sauce, dip or spread waiting for you in the fridge. With that in mind, I've created 15 "staple" recipes that can be made ahead of time and stored in the refrigerator for up to 5 days.

These recipes, found in the "In the Pantry" chapter, are meant not only to enrich the flavors of simple recipes but also to boost their nutritional content or add a more pleasing texture. The variety of these pantry recipes, from sweet to savory, provides a good base for successfully assembling any number of nutritious raw food meals in minutes. Recipes such as Creamy Alfredo Sauce (page 24) and Chunky Tomato Marinara Sauce (page 25) will heighten the flavor of your favorite vegetable pasta, and Berry Jam (page 31) makes a great addition to any healthy breakfast. One of my favorite recipes in a pinch is Quick Thai Cream Sauce (page 23); add some marinated thinly shaved vegetables and you have a complete meal in no time at all. By preparing these recipes ahead of time and keeping them on hand, you can jump-start delicious raw dishes and produce flavorful and nutritious results in a flash.

What constitutes a five-ingredient raw recipe that can be prepared in about 15 minutes? Since most people have salt and water readily on hand, I have not counted them among the five ingredients. Also, some of the more complex recipes call for an "In the Pantry" recipe as one of the ingredients. For some of those recipes I have provided an alternative should you not have a pantry recipe on hand.

The recipes in this book prove how simple and delicious raw food can be. And while all the dishes are wonderful on their own, pairing them up is an easy way to elevate your meals to gourmet level in minutes. For example, serve Mushroom "Fricassee" (page 168) on a bed of Cauliflower "Mashed Potatoes" (page 21), or dip Pecan Pie Brownies (page 200) in Chocolate Fondue (page 32). Whether you are a vegetarian, a vegan, a dedicated raw-foodist or a staunch meat-eater, you are sure to find fresh, flavorful dishes that will both appeal to your taste and leave you feeling full and satisfied.

From my kitchen to yours,
Chef Doug

Raw Food Know-How

What Is a Raw Food Diet?

A traditional raw food diet is vegetarian or vegan. The term *raw food* typically refers to any unprocessed whole food in its purest form. Uncooked avocados, apples, oranges and kale are all examples of raw food. Raw food cuisine is based on combining raw ingredients to create a dish. It can be as simple as Tomato, Parsley and Onion Salad (page 110) or as complex as Cranberry Hazelnut Cacao Crunch (page 41) drizzled with Chocolate Fondue (page 32) and finished with a dollop of Lemon Vanilla Cashew Yogurt (page 47).

A raw food diet contains whole, unprocessed fruits and vegetables, nuts and seeds and select legumes and grains that have not been heated past 105°F (41°C). Although there is some debate in the raw food community about what the maximum temperature should be, it is generally agreed that food should not be heated above this temperature.

Enzymes

All food in its whole, unprocessed form contains enzymes, which basically help plants to sustain life. Our bodies produce enzymes too — substances, usually proteins, that help to digest food, absorb nutrients and promote health, among other functions. Although there is a great deal of controversy regarding the relationship between food enzymes and health, those in the raw food community believe that when food is heated or cooked past 105°F (41°C), the natural enzymes begin to break down and the food loses a significant component of its nutritional value.

Organic Produce

Since most people are interested in raw food because of its health benefits, it is important to use organic produce whenever possible. Food that is grown organically has not been exposed to chemical fertilizers, herbicides or pesticides. At the very least, we do not know the long-term effects these chemicals have on our bodies. For the best-tasting, most nutritious food (because it is likely to be freshly picked or harvested), look for seasonal produce that has been grown locally by real farmers. In the short term it may be more expensive than food produced by agribusiness, but over the long term it is the most sustainable and healthful option.

To help you make informed food choices, the following list provided by the Environmental Working Group (www.ewg.org) — the "Dirty Dozen" — lists the 12 foods identified as being most contaminated by pesticide residues when not grown organically. Also listed are those that are least likely to be contaminated when not grown organically.

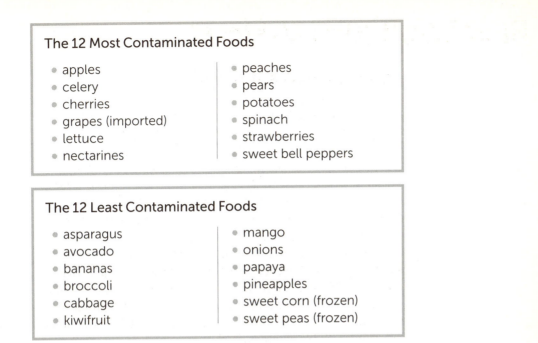

The 12 Most Contaminated Foods

- apples
- celery
- cherries
- grapes (imported)
- lettuce
- nectarines
- peaches
- pears
- potatoes
- spinach
- strawberries
- sweet bell peppers

The 12 Least Contaminated Foods

- asparagus
- avocado
- bananas
- broccoli
- cabbage
- kiwifruit
- mango
- onions
- papaya
- pineapples
- sweet corn (frozen)
- sweet peas (frozen)

Eating Raw in Cold Weather

One of the stigmas associated with raw food is that much of it is served at room temperature, cool or cold. While food temperature may not be an issue in warmer climates or during the summer, it can play a vital role in how we eat when it is cold outside. In chilly weather we tend to gravitate toward warmer foods because they feel comforting. When preparing or eating raw food, adding seasoning may help to compensate for the fact that it isn't warm.

For instance, studies show that adding a pinch of cayenne pepper or minced fresh chile pepper makes us feel warm by boosting our metabolic rate. Capsaicin, the substance in chiles that gives them their heat, also helps to improve digestion. Ginger is another ingredient that works to help us feel warmer in cooler months, and it too is an effective digestive aid.

And many recipes such as sauces and soups can be placed in a high-powered blender or food processor and processed for 45 to 60 seconds, until they are slightly warmed.

Five-Ingredient Recipes

In this book, I have created recipes that use five (or fewer) raw ingredients to create a dish. These recipes

- do not count salt or water as ingredients;
- may rely on recipes from the "In the Pantry" chapter to create more complex dishes, in which case that recipe is tallied as a single ingredient.

Tips for Transitioning to a Raw Food Diet

Transitioning to a raw food diet can seem overwhelming at first. Here are some quick and easy tips to get you going on your way.

- Start slowly. Approach your new diet day by day, slowly incorporating new elements and techniques as you progress.
- When going out to eat, have something before you leave. By eating beforehand you nourish your body with the foods you want to eat. This will also reduce the amount of explaining you need to do about why you are not eating much.
- When hunger hits, snack on a handful of unsalted raw almonds. They will provide protein, healthy fats and fiber and help to balance blood sugar levels.
- Do not be scared of healthy fats such as those provided by avocados, seeds and nuts. They leave you feeling nourished, and they can actually help you lose weight when consumed in moderation.
- When you crave sweets, try eating one or two dates. This will curb your craving and help you on your way toward eliminating processed sugars.
- If you are watching your sodium intake, try using dried kelp or dulse in a recipe instead of salt.
- Snack on fresh fruit throughout the day to keep blood sugar levels balanced.
- Replace your morning coffee with fresh juice.
- Keep berries in the freezer at all times so you can easily make a quick and nutritious smoothie.
- Drink smoothies regularly. As time goes by, start adding smoothies (or juices) that contain green vegetables.
- Write out a week-long meal plan before you go grocery shopping.
- As soon as you bring home your produce from the farmers' market or store, wash and store it for easy access.
- Search for an online community or join a group of other people transitioning to a raw food diet.
- Look for restaurants in your surrounding area that offer raw food classes, to gain a better understanding of a raw food diet.

Terms and Techniques for a Raw Vegan Kitchen

Juicing

Juicing is the process of running fruits, vegetables and/or herbs through a juicer, separating the liquid, which contains most of the nutrients, from the solids. Juicing is an important part of a raw food diet because it allows your body to assimilate nutrients more quickly and efficiently than when they are consumed as whole foods.

Soaking

Briefly soaking nuts and seeds in water before using makes blending, puréeing or grinding them easier and ensures the recipe yields a smooth result. Soaking in water also helps to remove any unwanted particles that may have come into contact with the food in the manufacturing process.

Marinating

Marinating is a common technique in raw food cuisine. It helps to break down raw fruits and vegetables, giving them the look and mouth-feel of being lightly cooked or steamed. Marinating foods such as carrots, beets, kale or any green vegetable for a short time can help make them seem more like cooked food.

Equipping a 15-Minute Raw Food Kitchen

You won't need a lot of special equipment to get started on a raw food diet. In fact, your kitchen probably already has most of what is required. For instance, a good **cutting board** is an important component of a raw food kitchen. One made of solid wood is ideal, as plastic will dull knives much more quickly. For convenience, buy a large board at least 2 feet (60 cm) long. If you are chopping a substantial amount of food, you can leave it in piles at the edges as completed and continue working seamlessly.

I recommend having at least two good **sharp knives**: a chef's knife for chopping and a paring knife for most other jobs. Since you will get the best results from many recipes by producing thin, even slices, I also suggest that you purchase a **mandoline**. This handy kitchen tool doesn't have to be expensive. It is essentially a blade attached to a frame that allows you to slice vegetables or fruits evenly and very thinly. I also recommend a **sharp-toothed grater**, such as those made by Microplane. This handy tool purées gingerroot and makes easy work of zesting citrus, which is used to enhance the flavor in many recipes.

If you don't already have one, you should also invest in a **colander**, a large strainer that can be placed in the sink. Soaked nuts and seeds are used widely in this book, and you'll need a colander for draining these foods. A fine-mesh sieve is helpful for straining small ingredients. You'll also need a good sturdy **vegetable peeler**. In addition to its obvious uses, this tool can be used for making raw "pasta" from vegetables such as carrots and zucchini (see page 145). There are two types of vegetable peelers: the more traditional type, with blades that run lengthwise, and a Y-shaped ("slingshot") version, which has blades across the top. The latter is the vegetable peeler of choice for raw cuisine because its shape allows you to peel long strips off vegetables with a continuous downward motion. When using a traditional vegetable peeler, you constantly need to reposition the blade, which can be time-consuming.

You'll certainly need a **blender** to make smoothies and many of the dips, sauces and dressings in this book. In addition to a blender, the only other somewhat expensive small appliance you'll need to get started is a **food processor**. Like a blender, it is used for puréeing and blending ingredients. The difference is that a food processor can handle denser foods and doesn't require as much liquid as a blender. You'll want a machine that has a capacity of at least 10 cups (2.5 L). The shredding and slicing blades that come with most models are very useful and can take the place of a mandoline for many jobs. A mini-bowl attachment is also helpful, for processing small quantities such as some dressings and sauces.

If you make the transition to a raw food diet, you should think about purchasing a **high-powered blender**. These machines have very powerful motors and have been designed so you can adjust the setting to achieve maximum results for specific tasks, such as making smoothies, sauces or dips. They are so powerful that they easily make a completely smooth purée of any nut, seed, vegetable or fruit. They can make delicious cream sauces or butters from soaked nuts; for some recipes it is simply not possible to achieve the ideal smooth, creamy consistency using a regular household blender.

Juicing plays an important role in raw food cuisine because fresh juices are very nutrient-dense. If you're transitioning to a raw food diet, I suggest that you consider investing in a **juicer** once you begin to consume lighter foods on a regular basis. Many different kinds of juicers are available. Read up on their features and look for one that fits your price range and meets your needs.

A **spiral vegetable slicer** (often referred to as a spiralizer) is a device used in raw food cuisine to make "pasta" from vegetables. These slicers come in different shapes and sizes and have a variety of blades. Depending on the brand you purchase, they can cut vegetables into pasta-like strands or paper-thin slices, and some will even make curlicues. The best prices are available online, but you can also look for them in natural foods stores, raw food specialty stores or, if you have one, your local Chinatown.

As you transition further into a raw food diet, you may want to invest in an **electric food dehydrator**, a kind of low-heat mini oven that enables you to soften foods and concentrate their flavors without destroying nutrients. It also allows you to create desirable textures in certain dishes. Electric food dehydrators are available at raw food specialty suppliers or online.

It is important to invest in **glass storage containers** when setting up a raw food kitchen. I also suggest that you use glass or stainless steel mixing bowls. Most plastic contains a substance called bisphenol A (BPA), which is now deemed a toxic substance and should be avoided whenever possible.

Stocking a 15-Minute Raw Food Pantry

Stocking a five-ingredient, 15-minute raw food pantry may seem somewhat tricky at first, but you'll find it's quite simple when you know what you are looking for. The following are some of the most commonly used ingredients in this book. Since the recipes use so few ingredients, try to purchase the most healthful products possible. When purchasing these ingredients, always be sure to look for products labeled "raw." If you have concerns, ask your purveyor.

Dried Herbs
- basil
- dill weed
- Italian seasoning
- oregano
- poultry seasoning

Spices
- cayenne pepper
- chili powder
- cinnamon
- cumin seeds (whole or ground)
- curry powder
- hot pepper flakes
- nutmeg (ground)
- smoked paprika
- sweet paprika
- turmeric (ground)

Cold-Pressed Oils
- extra virgin olive oil
- flax oil
- hemp oil
- sesame oil (untoasted)

Seasonings
- raw agave nectar
- apple cider vinegar (unpasteurized)
- brown rice miso (unpasteurized)
- mint extract (raw)
- nutritional yeast
- sea salt (fine)
- vanilla extract (raw)
- wheat-free tamari

Nuts
- almonds
- almond butter
- cashews
- hazelnuts
- pecans
- pistachios
- walnuts

Seeds
- chia seeds (white or dark)
- flax seeds (golden or brown)
- hemp seeds (shelled)
- pumpkin seeds
- sesame seeds
- sunflower seeds
- tahini

Coconut Products
- coconut butter
- coconut oil
- dried shredded coconut (unsulfured)

Other Ingredients
- apricots (dried)
- arame (dried)
- buckwheat groats
- cacao powder (raw)
- dates (Medjool)
- gingerroot
- nori
- raisins

In the Pantry
15 Raw Recipes to Make the Ordinary Extraordinary

Raw food cuisine, like other styles of cuisine, relies on standard recipes that are considered foundation or "mother" recipes. Recipes such as these are great for preparing delicious meals in a hurry, and I've created 15 of them specifically for this book. Each can be used as a base to create other dishes, as a garnish to finish a dish or simply on its own as part of a larger meal. All of them can be made ahead of time and kept in the refrigerator for up to five days.

Use these recipes to quickly transform everyday meals into something extraordinary. If you have Berry Jam (page 31) in the refrigerator, add a dollop to Breakfast Porridge (page 37). Drizzle some Mexican Fiesta Dressing (page 27) over Mexican Jicama Slaw (page 123). Top Carrot Pad Thai (page 150) with some tangy Quick Thai Cream Sauce (page 23). Add Chunky Tomato Marinara Sauce (page 25) and a sprinkle of hemp seeds to zucchini noodles. Use Sunflower Seed Hummus (page 29) as a dip or spread, or wrap it in a lettuce leaf or toss it with a salad for a protein-rich meal. Chocolate Fondue (page 32) is a wonderful addition to desserts — try it on Strawberry Coconut Shortcake Tart (page 203) or as a dip for Coconut Macaroons (page 201).

I've also included a recipe for Nut Milk (page 19). When you make your own nut milk, you control the ingredients — you know exactly what it contains. There is no added salt, sugar or hidden emulsifiers. It is raw, unpasteurized and a fraction of the cost of store-bought versions. While drinks such as Kiwi Coconut Lime Smoothie (page 60) and Peachy Plum Smoothie (page 54) work well made with water, replacing the water with nut milk makes them even more creamy, rich and delicious. Try blending nut milk with fresh berries for a sweet treat.

Many of the fruit-based drinks in this book use nut milk. Experimenting with these recipes will introduce you to the versatility of this wonderful refrigerator staple. Once you get comfortable making the recipes, you can use them as foundations to create original dishes of your own. For example, I often soak 1 cup (250 mL) raw cashews in 2 cups (500 mL) water for 30 minutes. After draining the cashews, I place them in a blender with about ½ cup (125 mL) Mexican Fiesta Dressing (page 27), ¼ cup (60 mL) filtered water and a pinch of fine sea salt. The result is creamy and rich Southwest Cashew Cream Sauce, which is wonderful served with shredded vegetables or some fresh carrot and celery sticks. The possibilities are endless!

Nut Milk

Most people do not realize how simple it is to make non-dairy milk at home. This recipe contains three ingredients and takes no more than five minutes to make.

Makes 4 cups (1 L)

Tips

Soaking the almonds will make the milk a bit creamier. If you have time, soak them for 30 minutes in 4 cups (1 L) warm water. When the soaking time has been completed, drain, discard the soaking liquid and rinse the almonds under cold running water until the water runs clear.

You can also strain the nut milk through cheesecloth or a nut-milk bag placed over a pitcher large enough to accommodate the liquid.

- **Fine mesh sieve**

1 cup	whole raw almonds (see Tips, left)	250 mL
4 cups	filtered water	1 L
Pinch	fine sea salt	Pinch

1. In a blender, combine almonds, water and salt. Blend at high speed for 45 seconds or until liquid becomes milky white and no visible pieces of almond remain.
2. Transfer to sieve and strain (see Tips, left). Serve immediately or cover and refrigerate for up to 3 days. Discard pulp or save for another use.

Variations

For slightly sweet nut milk, omit the salt and add a pinch of ground cinnamon and 1 or 2 pitted dates.

Almond Berry Milk: After processing the nut milk in Step 1, add 1 cup (250 mL) of your favorite berry (such as blueberries or strawberries) and blend at high speed until smooth.

Cashew Milk, Hazelnut Milk or Coconut Milk: Substitute an equal quantity of raw cashews, raw hazelnuts or unsweetened dried shredded coconut for the almonds.

Hemp Milk

Whether you have a nut allergy or are simply looking for something different, hemp milk is a great alternative to nut milk and easy to make at home. You can substitute hemp milk for nut milk in any of the recipes in this book.

Makes 4 cups (1 L)

3 tbsp	raw shelled hemp seeds	45 mL
4 cups	filtered water	1 L

In a blender, combine hemp seeds and water. (Shelled hemp seeds are soft and small enough to make straining unnecessary.) Serve immediately or cover and refrigerate for up to 3 days.

Herbed Cashew Cheese

Raw cuisine often uses the fats in nuts and seeds as a dairy replacement. This "cheese" is as creamy and filling as traditional cheese. Use it as a dip with fresh veggies or as a spread on crisp romaine lettuce leaves.

· ·

Makes
1¹⁄₂ cups (375 mL)

Tips

Substitute an equal quantity of pine nuts or macadamia nuts for the cashews. If using macadamia nuts, increase the water by 2 tbsp (30 mL).

Nutritional yeast flakes can be found in well-stocked supermarkets and natural foods stores. Although not a raw product, nutritional yeast is fortified with vitamin B$_{12}$. It helps to produce umami, the savory flavor that is sometimes lacking in vegetarian cuisine.

Substitute an equal amount of chopped fresh rosemary for the thyme.

2 cups	whole raw cashews (see Tips, left)	500 mL
¹⁄₂ cup	filtered water	125 mL
¹⁄₄ cup	freshly squeezed lemon juice	60 mL
¹⁄₄ cup	nutritional yeast (see Tips, left)	60 mL
4 tsp	chopped fresh thyme leaves (see Tips, left)	20 mL
1 tsp	fine sea salt	5 mL

1. In a food processor fitted with the metal blade, process cashews, water, lemon juice, nutritional yeast, thyme and salt until smooth, stopping motor to scrape down sides of work bowl as necessary. Transfer to a bowl. Serve immediately or cover and refrigerate for up to 4 days.

Cauliflower "Mashed Potatoes"

As a young man I loved to eat mashed potatoes with every meal. This delicious, dairy-free alternative is certain to please.

1 cup	whole raw cashews	250 mL
3 tbsp	nutritional yeast	45 mL
1 tsp	fine sea salt	5 mL
3 cups	chopped cauliflower (see Tips, left)	750 mL
3 tbsp	cold-pressed (extra virgin) olive oil	45 mL
1 tbsp	freshly squeezed lemon juice	15 mL

Makes 4 servings

Tips

Chopping the ingredients in a food processor before blending creates a smooth purée with very little liquid, ensuring a creamy result.

Remove the tougher stems from the cauliflower; they will not blend as well as the florets.

Cauliflower belongs to a group of vegetables called crucifers, which also includes arugula, broccoli, Brussels sprouts, kale and radishes. Crucifers contain cancer-fighting phytochemicals. These cancer fighters are very susceptible to high temperatures and are water-soluble, which means that their nutritional benefit is maximized when they are eaten raw.

1. In a food processor fitted with the metal blade, process cashews, nutritional yeast and salt until flour-like in consistency. Add cauliflower, olive oil and lemon juice. Process at high speed until finely chopped, stopping motor to scrape down sides of work bowl as necessary.

2. Transfer mixture to a blender and blend at high speed until smooth and creamy. Transfer to a bowl. Serve immediately or cover and refrigerate for up to 4 days.

Variations

For an even creamier dish, soak 2 cups (500 mL) whole raw cashews in 4 cups (1 L) warm water for 15 minutes. Drain, then add to ingredients in Step 2, along with an additional 1 cup (250 mL) chopped cauliflower florets and $\frac{1}{2}$ cup (125 mL) filtered water.

Herbed Cauliflower "Mashed Potatoes": In Step 2, add 1 tbsp (15 mL) chopped chives, 1 tsp (5 mL) chopped fresh rosemary and $\frac{1}{2}$ tsp (2 mL) chopped fresh thyme leaves.

Yellow Coconut Curry Sauce

One of my fondest memories of my first cooking job, in a British pub, is of the fragrant smell of a rich yellow coconut curry simmering on the stove. This raw curry sauce is delicious served with fresh zucchini noodles, marinated spinach or some raw cashews.

Makes
1 cup (250 mL)

Tips

Coconut oil is solid at room temperature but has a melting point of 76°F (24°C), so it is easy to liquefy. To melt it, place in a shallow glass bowl over a pot of simmering water.

Depending on the curry powder you use, this recipe can pack a punch. Add 2 tsp (10 mL) curry powder and then try a taste, adding more if you prefer.

½ cup	whole raw cashews	125 mL
½ cup	filtered water	125 mL
3 tbsp	melted coconut oil (see Tips, left)	45 mL
2 tsp to 1 tbsp	mild curry powder (see Tips, left)	10 to 15 mL
1 tbsp	freshly squeezed lemon juice	15 mL
1 tsp	chopped gingerroot (see Tip, below)	5 mL
½ tsp	fine sea salt	2 mL

1. In a blender, combine cashews, water, coconut oil, curry powder, lemon juice, ginger and salt. Blend at high speed until smooth. Transfer to a bowl. Serve immediately or cover and refrigerate for up to 5 days.

Variation

For a spicier flavor, add ¼ tsp (1 mL) cayenne pepper, or more if you prefer.

Teriyaki Sauce

I love the slightly sweet and salty kick you get from this sauce without using any refined sugars or oils. Try this with a handful of raw organic nuts or tossed with Vegetable "Fried Rice" (page 165).

Makes
⅔ cup (150 mL)

Tip

To remove the skin from fresh gingerroot with the least amount of waste, use the edge of a teaspoon. With a brushing motion, scrape off the skin to reveal the yellow root.

¼ cup	wheat-free tamari (see Tips, page 23)	60 mL
3 tbsp	raw agave nectar (see Tips, page 23)	45 mL
3 tbsp	sesame oil (untoasted)	45 mL
1 tbsp	chopped gingerroot (see Tip, left)	15 mL
½	clove garlic	½

1. In a blender, combine tamari, agave nectar, sesame oil, ginger and garlic. Blend at high speed until smooth. Transfer to a bowl. Serve immediately or cover and refrigerate for up to 7 days.

Quick Thai Cream Sauce

Thai food is renowned for its sweet, salty, spicy and sour flavor profile. This rich and creamy sauce blends those flavors and makes a perfect addition to any dish. Try it with Carrot Pad Thai (page 150) garnished with a wedge of lime and some crushed Teriyaki Almonds (page 93).

	Makes
Makes	
1¼ cups (300 mL)	

Tips

A 2 tbsp (30 mL) serving of almond butter contains about 190 calories. In addition to being a good source of protein, it is high in phosphorus and a source of calcium, potassium and fiber. Although it's high in calories, you don't need a large amount to feel full.

Coconut oil is solid at room temperature but has a melting point of 76°F (24°C), so it is easy to liquefy. To melt it, place in a shallow glass bowl over a pot of simmering water.

When purchasing agave nectar, be sure to look for products labeled "raw." Most agave nectar on the market has been heated to a high temperature and so does not qualify as raw food. If you have concerns, ask your purveyor.

Although not a raw product, wheat-free tamari is gluten-free. If you are following a strictly raw diet, try using nama shoyu, an unpasteurized version of tamari, but keep in mind that it does contain gluten.

½ cup	raw almond butter (see Tips, left)	125 mL
¼ cup	filtered water	60 mL
3 tbsp	freshly squeezed lime juice	45 mL
2 tbsp	melted coconut oil (see Tips, left)	30 mL
2 tbsp	raw agave nectar (see Tips, left)	30 mL
2 tbsp	wheat-free tamari (see Tips, left)	30 mL

1. In a blender, combine almond butter, water, lime juice, coconut oil, agave nectar and tamari. Blend at high speed until smooth. Transfer to a bowl. Serve immediately or cover and refrigerate for up to 5 days.

Variations

For a nut-free version, substitute an equal amount of raw pumpkin seed butter for the raw almond butter.

For a spicy kick, add ¼ tsp (1 mL) cayenne pepper.

Creamy Alfredo Sauce

Traditionally Alfredo sauce is made using heavy cream, butter and cheese. My version of this classic uses cashews to create the creamy texture and nutritional yeast to replace the flavor of cheese. Enjoy this sauce with Celery Root Ravioli (page 147) or Stuffed Mushroom Caps (page 167), or simply tossed with some fresh zucchini noodles.

1 cup	whole raw cashews, soaked (see Tips, left)	250 mL
1 cup	filtered water	250 mL
3 tbsp to ¼ cup	nutritional yeast (see Tips, left)	45 to 60 mL
2 tbsp	freshly squeezed lemon juice	30 mL
1 tsp	fine sea salt	5 mL
½	clove garlic	½

Makes
1½ cups (375 mL)

Tips

To soak the cashews, place them in a bowl with 2 cups (500 mL) warm water. Cover and set aside for 10 minutes. Drain, discarding soaking liquid. Rinse under cold running water until the water runs clear.

Nutritional yeast flakes can be found in well-stocked supermarkets and natural foods stores. Although not a raw product, nutritional yeast is fortified with vitamin B_{12}. It helps to produce umami, the savory flavor sometimes lacking in vegetarian cuisine.

The nutritional yeast in this sauce creates a strong umami flavor, which most people enjoy. However, if you are sensitive to strong flavors, reduce the quantity, to taste.

1. In a blender, combine soaked cashews, water, nutritional yeast, lemon juice, salt and garlic. Blend at high speed until smooth. Serve immediately or cover and refrigerate for up to 5 days.

Variation

If you do not have nutritional yeast, you can substitute 2 tsp (10 mL) brown rice miso, which is gluten-free, and reduce the amount of salt to ½ tsp (2 mL). Miso is a good substitution because it also adds an umami flavor to the sauce.

Chunky Tomato Marinara Sauce

Serve this sauce, a perfect blend of ripe, juicy tomatoes and fragrant basil, with Cashew Almond Gnocchi (page 149) or Spaghetti and Seed Balls (page 143). It's also delicious added to Zucchini Spaghetti with Lemon and Herbs (page 144).

**Makes
3 cups (750 mL)**

Tips

Any variety of tomato will work well in this recipe. Try Roma, hothouse or heirloom tomatoes — just make sure they are ripe.

Substitute 1 tbsp (15 mL) dried basil for the fresh basil.

To remove the skin from a clove of garlic, use the butt end of a chef's knife to press firmly but gently on the clove to loosen the skin. Using your index finger and thumb, carefully ease off the skin.

1½ cups	chopped tomatoes (see Tips, left)	375 mL
½ cup	fresh basil leaves (see Tips, left)	125 mL
¼ cup	cold-pressed (extra virgin) olive oil	60 mL
2 tbsp	freshly squeezed lemon juice	30 mL
½ tsp	fine sea salt	2 mL
2	cloves garlic (see Tips, left)	2

1. In a food processor fitted with the metal blade, process tomatoes, basil, olive oil, lemon juice, salt and garlic until smooth, stopping motor to scrape down sides of work bowl as necessary. Transfer to a bowl. Serve immediately or cover and refrigerate for up to 4 days.

Green Pesto

Pesto is one of the most versatile recipes. Use it as a dip for fresh vegetables, as a spread on a sandwich, as a sauce for a main dish or as flavoring for a soup or sauce. In a few simple steps you can make pesto at home in no time.

Makes 2 cups (500 mL)

Tip

Walnuts provide alpha-linolenic acid (ALA), the omega-3 fat that is an essential fatty acid — without it, we could not survive. It is called "essential" because our bodies are unable to make it and we must obtain it from food. Other good sources of ALA include flax and chia seeds. Research has demonstrated ALA's ability to reduce chronic inflammation and other risk factors for diabetes, heart disease and stroke. It is estimated that North Americans get on average about 1.5 grams of ALA per day, while some experts recommend an intake of 2.3 to 3 grams per day. Reaching this goal is easy if you make ALA-rich foods part of your daily diet.

4 cups	roughly chopped flat-leaf (Italian) parsley leaves	1 L
½ cup	cold-pressed (extra virgin) olive oil	125 mL
½ cup	raw walnut halves (see Tip, left)	125 mL
¼ cup	freshly squeezed lemon juice	60 mL
½ tsp	fine sea salt	2 mL
3	cloves garlic (see Tips, page 25)	3

1. In a food processor fitted with the metal blade, process parsley, olive oil, walnuts, lemon juice, salt and garlic until smooth, stopping motor and scraping down sides of work bowl as necessary. Transfer to a bowl. Serve immediately or cover and refrigerate for up to 5 days.

Variations

Omit the walnuts and increase the parsley to 6 cups (1.5 L) and the olive oil to ¾ cup (175 mL).

Substitute an equal amount of fresh cilantro for the parsley or an equal amount of raw shelled hemp seeds for the walnuts.

Mexican Fiesta Dressing

Inspired by the bold flavors of Mexican cuisine, this dressing adds fresh, spicy flavor to any dish. Try adding it to sauces such as Creamy Alfredo Sauce (page 24) or to salad dressings such as Lemon Tahini Dressing (page 131), or use it to garnish Summer Corn Cakes (page 162), Sweet Potato Enchilada (page 160) or Squash Burrito (page 159).

• •

Makes
1¼ cups (300 mL)

Tips

To ensure that any grit is removed from your parsley before chopping, place it in a bowl, cover with cool water and set aside for 2 minutes. The dirt will sink to the bottom of the bowl. Lift out the parsley, rinse under running water and pat dry.

I prefer to use organic sea salt. This type of salt is classified as a whole food and is said to contain many trace minerals. If salt intake is something you are concerned about, feel free to use less than called for or omit it completely.

1	bunch flat-leaf (Italian) parsley leaves, roughly chopped (see Tips, left)	1
½ cup	cold-pressed (extra virgin) olive oil	125 mL
½ cup	filtered water	125 mL
¼ cup	freshly squeezed lemon juice	60 mL
3 tbsp	chili powder	45 mL
2 tbsp	ground cumin	30 mL
1 tsp	fine sea salt (see Tips, left)	5 mL

1. In a food processor fitted with the metal blade, process parsley, olive oil, water, lemon juice, chili powder, cumin and salt until smooth, stopping motor to scrape down sides of work bowl as necessary. Transfer to a bowl. Serve immediately or cover and refrigerate for up to 5 days.

Variation

Substitute 2 bunches of fresh cilantro leaves, roughly chopped, for the parsley.

Tahini Tzatziki

Many raw recipes achieve a rich, creamy flavor similar to that of dairy by using high-quality nuts or seeds. This creamy tzatziki is one of my favorites.

**Makes
1¼ cups (300 mL)**

Tips

Use the large holes of a box grater to shred the cucumber. If you are using an English cucumber, you do not need to peel off the skin or remove the seeds before shredding. If you are using a field cucumber, you must remove the tough skin and the seeds, as they can be bitter. To remove the seeds, cut the cucumber in half lengthwise and, using a spoon, scoop out and discard them.

To grate the garlic for this recipe, use a sharp-toothed grater such as those made by Microplane. Feel free to increase the amount of garlic to as many as 5 cloves.

In Step 2 you may substitute ¼ cup (60 mL) roughly chopped fresh dill fronds for the dried dill weed.

½ cup	peeled, seeded, shredded cucumber (see Tips, left)	125 mL
¾ tsp	fine sea salt, divided	3 mL
⅓ cup	raw tahini (see Tip, page 29)	75 mL
3 tbsp	filtered water	45 mL
3 tbsp	freshly squeezed lemon juice	45 mL
1 tsp	dried dill weed (see Tips, left)	5 mL
2½	cloves garlic, divided	2½

1. In a bowl, combine cucumber and ¼ tsp (1 mL) salt. Mix well. Cover and set aside for 5 minutes so the salt can draw out some of the moisture from the cucumber.

2. In a blender, combine tahini, ½ tsp (2 mL) salt, water, lemon juice, dill weed and ½ clove garlic. Blend at high speed until smooth.

3. Remove cucumber from bowl and, using your hands, squeeze out and discard remaining liquid. Return cucumber to bowl and stir in tahini mixture. Grate remaining garlic into mixture (see Tips, left). Stir well. Serve immediately or cover and refrigerate for up to 4 days.

Sunflower Seed Hummus

I love the rich, creamy flavor of hummus, but it is too high in fat for me to enjoy every day. This simple, high-protein alternative uses sunflower seeds with no added oils.

● ●

Makes
2 cups (500 mL)

Tip

Tahini is a paste or butter made from ground sesame seeds that is similar to peanut or almond butter. Most store-bought tahini is made from sesame seeds that have been roasted, depriving it of its raw status. If you are following a strictly raw diet, be sure to look for products labeled "raw." If you have concerns, ask your purveyor.

1½ cups	raw sunflower seeds	375 mL
⅓ cup	freshly squeezed lemon juice	75 mL
¼ cup	filtered water	60 mL
3 tbsp	wheat-free tamari (see Tips, page 30)	45 mL
3 tbsp	raw tahini (see Tip, left)	45 mL
½	clove garlic	½

1. In a food processor fitted with the metal blade, process sunflower seeds, lemon juice, water, tamari, tahini and garlic until smooth, stopping motor and scraping down sides of work bowl as necessary. Transfer to a bowl. Serve immediately or cover and refrigerate for up to 5 days.

Variations

For a fresh herb flavor, add 1 tbsp (15 mL) dried dill weed.

Thai Sunflower Hummus: Substitute freshly squeezed lime juice for the lemon juice and add 1 tbsp (15 mL) raw agave nectar and ¼ tsp (1 mL) cayenne pepper.

Spiced Nut Crumble

Protein makes you feel full and is a necessary part of everyone's diet. This spicy crumble can be used to top a salad, stuff a collard leaf or mix into a slaw for a quick and delicious hit of protein.

....

**Makes
1 cup (250 mL)**

Tips

Walnuts provide omega-3 fats, which are essential for overall health and well-being. They help to reduce inflammation and other risk factors for diabetes, heart disease and stroke. Include foods rich in omega-3 fats, such as walnuts, chia and flax, in your diet every day.

Substitute an equal amount of sweet smoked paprika for the chili powder.

While wheat-free tamari is not raw, it is gluten-free. The raw alternative for tamari, nama shoyu, does contain gluten. If you are following a completely raw diet and can tolerate gluten, by all means substitute an equal amount of nama shoyu.

2 cups	raw walnut halves (see Tips, left)	500 mL
$\frac{1}{2}$ tsp	chili powder (see Tips, left)	2 mL
2 tbsp	cold-pressed (extra virgin) olive oil	30 mL
1 tbsp	wheat-free tamari (see Tips, left)	15 mL

1. In a food processor fitted with the metal blade, process walnuts and chili powder until roughly chopped (you want to retain some texture).
2. Add olive oil and tamari. Pulse 8 to 10 times or just until combined. Transfer to a bowl. Serve immediately or cover and refrigerate for up to 5 days.

Variation

Sweet Nut Crumble: Substitute an equal amount of ground cinnamon for the chili powder, raw agave nectar for the olive oil, and $\frac{1}{4}$ tsp (1 mL) raw vanilla extract for the tamari.

Berry Jam

Most commercial jams are full of added sugars and preservatives. This jam is pure, sweet and versatile. Use it as a spread or to sweeten a dessert or smoothie.

**Makes
2 cups (500 mL)**

Tips

When purchasing raw vanilla extract, look for alcohol-free extract, to avoid the taste of raw alcohol in your dish.

For a sweeter jam, add more raw agave nectar, 1 tbsp (15 mL) at a time, until it suits your taste.

When soaked, chia seeds can swell up to nine times their original size. This typically takes between 10 and 15 minutes, so be patient when working with these seeds.

3 cups	hulled strawberries	750 mL
2 tbsp	warm filtered water	30 mL
1/4 tsp	raw vanilla extract (see Tips, left)	1 mL
1/4 cup	raw agave nectar (see Tips, left)	60 mL
1/4 cup	ground chia seeds (see Tips, left)	60 mL
1 tbsp	whole chia seeds	15 mL

1. In a food processor fitted with the metal blade, process strawberries, water, vanilla and agave nectar until smooth, stopping motor and scraping down sides of work bowl as necessary. Transfer to a bowl.

2. Add ground and whole chia seeds and mix well. Cover and set aside for about 10 minutes so the chia seeds can absorb the liquid and swell. Serve immediately or cover and refrigerate for up to 5 days.

Variations

Try substituting an equal amount of blueberries, raspberries or blackberries for the strawberries.

I like to add 2 tsp (10 mL) orange zest and a pinch of cinnamon to this jam.

Chocolate Fondue

This rich, chocolaty fondue is perfect as a dessert topping, as a dip for fresh fruit or simply for licking off the spoon.

Makes
1¼ cups (300 mL)

Tips

Coconut oil is solid at room temperature but has a melting point of 76°F (24°C), so it is easy to liquefy. To melt it, place in a shallow glass bowl over a pot of simmering water.

Cacao powder is powdered raw chocolate. It is similar to cocoa powder but tastes even better, with a deeper, richer flavor. Cacao powder is available in well-stocked supermarkets and natural foods stores and online. If you are transitioning to a raw food diet and can't find it, you may substitute an equal quantity of good-quality cocoa powder, but note that the beans in cocoa powder have been roasted, depriving them of their raw status. If you are following a strictly raw diet, use cacao powder.

When purchasing agave nectar, be sure to look for products labeled "raw." Most of the agave nectar on the market has been heated to a high temperature and so does not qualify as raw food. If you have concerns, ask your purveyor.

½ cup	melted coconut oil (see Tips, left)	125 mL
½ cup	raw cacao powder (see Tips, left)	125 mL
⅓ cup	raw agave nectar (see Tips, left)	75 mL
1 tbsp	cool filtered water	15 mL
Dash	raw vanilla extract	Dash

1. In a blender, combine coconut oil, cacao powder, agave nectar, water and vanilla. Blend at high speed until smooth. Transfer to a bowl. Serve immediately or cover and store at room temperature for up to 5 days.

Breakfast

When we think of breakfast, most of us imagine traditional wheat-based and sugar-rich foods such as toast, bagels, pancakes, jams and spreads. However, there are many other options for our first meal of the day.

Try a nutrient-dense smoothie such as Blueberry Banana Cream Smoothie (page 52) or Kiwi Coconut Lime Smoothie (page 60), or a fresh juice such as Beet Me Green Juice (page 88). If you feel you need a bit more protein in your morning smoothie, add one or two scoops of your favorite raw protein powder or 2 to 3 tbsp (30 to 45 mL) raw shelled hemp seeds.

While I love smoothies and fresh organic juices in the morning, sometimes I want to eat something crunchy or more substantial. Cinnamon Crunch Cereal (page 40) and Cranberry Hazelnut Cacao Crunch (page 41) will keep you feeling full until lunch. Date Muesli (page 44) and Rise and Shine Bars (page 45) are nutrient-dense and rich in protein — perfect for making ahead to grab on the go.

When making raw breakfast bowls, I like to add flavor by drizzling a sauce or a dollop of spread on top. Try Lemon Vanilla Cashew Yogurt (page 47), Orange Marmalade (page 47) or Chocolate Fondue (page 32) on Breakfast Porridge (page 37) or Almond Ginger Apple Hemp Cereal (page 39) for sweet and delicious variations.

Nutritionists often say that breakfast is the most important meal of the day, and I agree. Try these recipes and get off to a good start with a balance of healthy fats, proteins and carbohydrates.

Chocolate Berry Pudding

This rich, chocolaty, nutritious breakfast takes only a few minutes to prepare. Make it on days when you are strapped for time.

**Makes
1 main-course or
2 side servings**

Tip

The chia seeds in this recipe are used to add a slightly crunchy texture to the pudding, so they do not need to be soaked. Because they are so small, chia seeds can be consumed without soaking or grinding. When soaked, they absorb liquid and swell quickly.

1¼ cups	filtered water	300 mL
3 tbsp	chia seeds (see Tip, left)	45 mL
2 tbsp	raw agave nectar	30 mL
2 tbsp	raw cacao powder (see Tips, page 36)	30 mL
¼ tsp	raw vanilla extract	1 mL
¼ cup	fresh blueberries, strawberries or raspberries	60 mL

1. In a blender, combine water, chia seeds, agave nectar, cacao powder and vanilla. Blend at high speed until smooth. Transfer to a serving bowl and top with fresh berries. Serve immediately or cover and refrigerate for up to 2 days.

Variations

For a sweeter dish, substitute an equal amount of freshly squeezed orange juice for the water.

For a boost of protein, serve with 2 tbsp (30 mL) raw shelled hemp seeds, a few raw walnuts and a dollop of Lemon Vanilla Cashew Yogurt (page 47).

Banana Cinnamon Pudding: Substitute 2 tsp (10 mL) ground cinnamon for the cacao powder and ½ cup (125 mL) chopped banana for the fresh berries. To finish, top with an additional ½ cup (125 mL) chopped banana.

Easy Chocolate Chia

This smooth and chocolaty breakfast can be made a day in advance and left in the refrigerator for a quick meal on the go. Don't be fooled by the rich and sinful flavor — it's actually very good for you.

Makes 1 serving

Tips

Cacao powder is powdered raw chocolate. It is similar to cocoa powder but tastes even better, with a deeper, richer flavor. Cacao powder is available in well-stocked supermarkets, natural foods stores and online. If you are transitioning to a raw foods diet and can't find it, substitute an equal quantity of good-quality cocoa powder.

Either white or black chia seeds work well in this recipe.

1 cup	filtered water	250 mL
1/4 cup	raw cacao powder (see Tips, left)	60 mL
2 tbsp	raw agave nectar	30 mL
1 tsp	raw shelled hemp seeds	5 mL
1/8 tsp	raw vanilla extract	0.5 mL
2 tbsp	chia seeds (see Tips, left)	30 mL

1. In a blender, combine water, cacao powder, agave nectar, hemp seeds and vanilla. Blend at high speed until smooth.

2. In a bowl, whisk together chia seeds and cacao mixture until well combined. Cover and set aside for about 10 minutes so the chia seeds can absorb the liquid and swell. Serve immediately or cover and refrigerate for up to 2 days.

Variations

For a creamier pudding, substitute an equal amount of Nut Milk (page 19) for the water.

For added crunch and protein, add 1/4 cup (60 mL) whole raw almonds and 2 tbsp (30 mL) whole raw cashews.

Breakfast Porridge

A crunchy blend of nutrient-dense seeds makes this porridge a great way to start your day.

Makes 1 serving

Tips

When soaked, chia seeds can swell up to nine times their original size. This typically takes between 10 and 15 minutes, so be patient when working with these seeds.

When purchasing agave nectar, be sure to look for products labeled "raw." Most of the agave nectar on the market has been heated to a high temperature and so does not qualify as raw food. If you have concerns, ask your purveyor.

When purchasing raw vanilla extract, look for alcohol-free extract, to avoid the taste of raw alcohol in your dish.

1 cup	filtered water	250 mL
¼ cup	raw pumpkin seeds	60 mL
3 tbsp	chia seeds (see Tips, left)	45 mL
3 tbsp	raw agave nectar (see Tips, left)	45 mL
2 tbsp	raw shelled hemp seeds	30 mL
¼ tsp	raw vanilla extract (see Tips, left)	1 mL

1. In a bowl, combine water, pumpkin seeds, chia seeds, agave nectar, hemp seeds and vanilla. Mix well. Cover and set aside for about 10 minutes so the chia seeds can absorb the liquid and swell. Serve immediately or cover and refrigerate for up to 2 days.

Variations

I like to add a dash of ground cinnamon and freshly grated nutmeg right before serving.

For a creamier dish, substitute an equal amount of Nut Milk (page 19) for the water.

Substitute an equal amount of Coconut Milk (page 19, Variations) for the water, whole raw almonds for the pumpkin seeds, and raw sesame seeds for the hemp seeds.

Easy Almond Banana "Oatmeal"

This nutrient-dense breakfast is best enjoyed with a drizzle of raw agave nectar, a little Berry Jam (page 31) and some Chocolate Fondue (page 32).

Makes 1 serving

Tips

Substitute an equal amount of whole raw cashews for the almonds.

When a recipe calls for flax seeds, you have two options to choose from: golden or brown. They are basically interchangeable except for the effect they have on the color of the product. Golden seeds produce a lighter shade of brown.

Substitute ¼ cup (60 mL) melted coconut oil for the coconut butter.

¾ cup	whole raw almonds (see Tips, left)	175 mL
3 tbsp	ground flax seeds (see Tips, left)	45 mL
½ cup	chopped banana (about 1 medium)	125 mL
3 tbsp	coconut butter (see Tips, left)	45 mL
2 tbsp	raw agave nectar	30 mL

1. In a food processor fitted with the metal blade, process almonds until flour-like in consistency. Add flax seeds and pulse 2 to 3 times to combine. Add banana, coconut butter and agave nectar and process until smooth. Serve immediately or cover and refrigerate for up to 2 days.

Variations

For a bit of extra flavor, add ¼ tsp (1 mL) ground cinnamon and a dash of raw vanilla extract.

Almond Banana Berry Porridge: Add ½ cup (125 mL) blueberries and ¼ cup (60 mL) hulled strawberries along with the banana.

Almond Ginger Apple Hemp Cereal

I love this cereal — it's an aromatic spicy, sweet and crunchy blend of apples, ginger, cinnamon and hemp seeds. I like to take it with me on mornings when I am on the go.

Makes 1 serving

Tips

I like to use Royal Gala or McIntosh apples because they have a higher sugar content. If you are watching your sugar intake, feel free to use Granny Smiths, but keep in mind that the cereal will taste a little tarter.

To remove the skin from fresh gingerroot with the least amount of waste, use the edge of a teaspoon. With a brushing motion, scrape off the skin to reveal the yellow root.

Use high-quality organic cinnamon. You will get the freshest flavor by grinding whole cinnamon sticks in a spice grinder.

2 cups	peeled, chopped apples (see Tips, left)	500 mL
½ cup	whole raw almonds	125 mL
¼ cup	chopped gingerroot (see Tips, left)	60 mL
¼ cup	filtered water	60 mL
1 tsp	ground cinnamon (see Tips, left)	5 mL
¼ cup	raw shelled hemp seeds	60 mL

1. In a food processor fitted with the metal blade, process apples, almonds, ginger, water and cinnamon until roughly chopped (you want to retain some texture). Transfer to a serving bowl and top with hemp seeds. Serve immediately.

Variations

For a creamier dish, substitute an equal amount of fresh Nut Milk (page 19) for the water.

I like to garnish this with 2 to 3 tbsp (30 to 45 mL) each raw pumpkin seeds and raw sunflower seeds.

Cinnamon Crunch Cereal

This raw vegan breakfast bowl is loaded with healthy proteins, fats and fiber, which will keep you feeling full well into the lunch hour.

Makes 1 serving

Tips

Be sure to use raw buckwheat groats, not kasha, which has been toasted.

If you make this recipe ahead of time and refrigerate it, the buckwheat will absorb the liquid and swell. You will need to add 1/4 to 1/2 cup (60 to 125 mL) more liquid before serving.

Almonds are very nutritious. They include phytochemicals, protein, fiber and healthy fats, as well as vitamin E, magnesium, phosphorus, potassium, manganese and a small amount of B vitamins.

1/2 cup	filtered water	125 mL
1/4 cup	buckwheat groats (see Tips, left)	60 mL
1/4 cup	whole raw almonds (see Tips, left)	60 mL
3 tbsp	raw pumpkin seeds	45 mL
3 tbsp	raw agave nectar	45 mL
1/2 tsp	ground cinnamon	2 mL

1. In a serving bowl, combine water, buckwheat, almonds, pumpkin seeds, agave nectar and cinnamon. Serve immediately or cover and refrigerate for up to 2 days.

Variations

For a creamier dish, substitute an equal amount of Nut Milk (page 19) for the water.

Substitute whole raw cashews, raw pine nuts or raw walnut halves for the almonds.

Chocolate Crunch Cereal: Replace the ground cinnamon with 2 tbsp (30 mL) raw cacao powder.

Buckwheat Groats

Cinnamon Crunch Cereal is just one way of using raw buckwheat groats as a base for a bowl. I also drown them in Nut Milk (page 19) or water and add a pinch of ground cinnamon, some raw pumpkin seeds, raw shelled hemp seeds and fresh fruit. For some sweetness I add a drizzle of raw agave nectar or a few chopped dates. You will find that buckwheat leaves you feeling full because it is high in both fiber and protein.

Cranberry Hazelnut Cacao Crunch

The combination of sweet and tart flavors in this simple breakfast is sure to please even the pickiest of eaters. I enjoy this with a tall glass of cold Nut Milk (page 19).

Makes 1 serving

Tips

You may substitute an equal quantity of raw walnut halves or whole raw cashews for the hazelnuts, but keep in mind that hazelnuts provide more crunch than walnuts and cashews.

Cacao powder is powdered raw chocolate. It is similar to cocoa powder but tastes even better, with a deeper, richer flavor. Cacao powder is available in well-stocked supermarkets and natural foods stores and online. If you are transitioning to a raw food diet and can't find it, you may substitute an equal quantity of good-quality cocoa powder, but note that the beans in cocoa powder have been roasted, depriving them of their raw status. If you are following a strictly raw diet, use cacao powder.

¼ cup	whole raw hazelnuts (see Tips, left)	60 mL
3 tbsp	raw cacao powder (see Tips, left)	45 mL
¼ cup	raw agave nectar, divided	60 mL
½ cup	freshly squeezed orange juice	125 mL
¼ cup	cranberries	60 mL

1. In a food processor fitted with the metal blade, process hazelnuts and cacao powder until nuts are coarsely chopped. Add 3 tbsp (45 mL) agave nectar and pulse 7 to 8 times, until nuts begin to stick together. Transfer to a bowl.
2. Add orange juice, cranberries and remaining 1 tbsp (15 mL) agave nectar to food processor work bowl and process until smooth. Transfer to a serving bowl and top with hazelnut mixture. Serve immediately or cover and refrigerate for up to 2 days.

Variation

Substitute an equal amount of raspberries for the cranberries.

Blueberry Granola Bowl

This breakfast bowl is a blend of fresh blueberries, soft hemp seeds, sweet dates and crunchy almonds. Make this ahead of time and leave it in the fridge overnight for a quick morning meal.

Tip

There are numerous varieties of dates, but Medjool is my favorite. Although they are generally more expensive, they are larger, softer and ideal for using in raw food recipes.

¼ cup	raw shelled hemp seeds, divided	60 mL
1 cup	filtered water	250 mL
2 tbsp	raw agave nectar	30 mL
½ cup	whole raw almonds	125 mL
¼ cup	fresh blueberries	60 mL
2 tbsp	chopped pitted dates (see Tip, left)	30 mL

1. In a blender, combine 2 tbsp (30 mL) hemp seeds and water. Blend until smooth. Set aside.
2. In a food processor fitted with the metal blade, process almonds until broken down but not flour-like in consistency. Transfer to a serving bowl.
3. Add blended hemp seed mixture, remaining 2 tbsp (30 mL) hemp seeds, blueberries and dates and stir until well combined. Serve immediately or cover and refrigerate for up to 2 days.

Variation

Tropical Granola Bowl: Substitute 1 cup chopped mango (250 mL), divided, for the blueberries. In Step 1, add ½ cup (125 mL) chopped mango to the blender. In Step 3, substitute remaining ½ cup (125 mL) chopped mango for the blueberries. I also like to add ¼ cup (60 mL) each chopped papaya and pineapple.

Buckwheat Berry Bowl

This berry bowl is a fresh and simple breakfast that is not only delicious but also filling. Try serving this with a Kiwi Coconut Lime Smoothie (page 60).

(page 60)

Makes 1 serving

Tips

Be sure to use buckwheat groats, not kasha, which has been toasted.

To soak the buckwheat groats, place in a bowl with 2 cups (500 mL) water. Cover and set aside for 15 minutes. Drain, discarding soaking water, and rinse under cold running water until the water runs clear.

1/3 cup	buckwheat groats, soaked (see Tips, left)	75 mL
1/4 cup	filtered water	60 mL
1/4 cup	raw agave nectar	60 mL
2 tbsp	freshly squeezed lemon juice	30 mL
1 cup	blueberries, divided	250 mL
1/2 cup	hulled strawberries	125 mL

1. In a food processor fitted with the metal blade, process soaked buckwheat, water, agave nectar, lemon juice, 1/2 cup (125 mL) blueberries and strawberries until smooth, stopping motor once and scraping down sides of work bowl.
2. Transfer to a serving bowl and stir in remaining 1/2 cup (125 mL) blueberries. Serve immediately or cover and refrigerate for up to 2 days.

Variation

Chocolate Buckwheat Berry Bowl: In step 1, add 2 tbsp (30 mL) raw cacao powder and increase the agave nectar to 3 tbsp (45 mL).

Date Muesli

I find myself making this recipe when my body craves protein after a hard workout at the gym. I like the mixture of chunky rich nuts and seeds blended with sweet dates.

¼ cup	whole raw almonds	60 mL
¼ cup	whole raw cashews	60 mL
2 tbsp	raw pumpkin seeds	30 mL
1 tbsp	raw sunflower seeds	15 mL
¼ cup	chopped pitted dates (see Tips, page 45)	60 mL
½ cup	filtered water	125 mL

Makes 1 serving

1. In a food processor fitted with the metal blade, process almonds, cashews, pumpkin seeds and sunflower seeds until roughly chopped. Add dates and pulse 8 to 10 times, until combined.
2. Transfer to a serving bowl and add water. Serve immediately or cover and refrigerate for up to 2 days.

Tips

If you want to make this ahead and keep it on hand for a quick, nutritious breakfast, omit the water and store in an airtight container at room temperature for up to 5 days. Add ½ cup filtered water before serving.

Almonds are very nutritious. They include phytochemicals, protein, fiber and healthy fats, as well as vitamin E, magnesium, phosphorus, potassium, manganese and a small amount of B vitamins.

Variations

For a creamier dish, substitute an equal amount of fresh Nut Milk (page 19) for the water.

Try topping this with a dollop of Lemon Vanilla Cashew Yogurt (page 47), a pinch of ground cinnamon and a dash of raw agave nectar.

Replace the dates with ½ cup (125 mL) raisins soaked in warm water for 10 minutes.

Rise and Shine Bars

Most of us have very little time to make breakfast. These nutrient-dense bars are easy to make well ahead of time and can be stored in the refrigerator for up to a week.

Makes 10 to 12 bars

Tips

There are numerous varieties of dates, but Medjool is my favorite. Although they are generally more expensive, Medjool dates are larger, softer and ideal for using in raw food recipes.

Dates make a great base when combined with raw nuts, seeds or other dried fruits in a food processor. Try adding sunflower seeds, pumpkin seeds, pine nuts or even walnuts.

2 cups	chopped pitted dates (see Tips, left)	500 mL
1/2 cup	whole raw almonds	125 mL
1/4 cup	whole raw cashews	60 mL
1/4 cup	raw shelled hemp seeds	60 mL
2 tsp	finely grated orange zest	10 mL

1. In a food processor fitted with the metal blade, process dates, almonds, cashews, hemp seeds and orange zest until well combined. Transfer to a bowl.
2. Using a 1/4-cup (60 mL) measuring cup, divide mixture into 10 to 12 equal portions. Using your hands, form into bars approximately 3 inches (7.5 cm) long and 1 inch (2.5 cm) wide. Serve immediately or cover and refrigerate for up to 7 days.

Variations

Substitute an equal amount of lemon zest for the orange zest.

Chocolate Energy Bars: Substitute 1/4 cup (60 mL) raw cacao powder for the lemon zest and add 3 tbsp (45 mL) raw agave nectar in Step 1.

Cashew Scramble Wrap

This tasty wrap is a play on the traditional breakfast burrito but without any of the cholesterol, refined sugars or flours. Rich and creamy cashews marry well with the fresh bite of the collard greens and flavorful red pepper.

Makes 1 serving

Tips

To soak the cashews, place in a bowl with 2 cups (500 mL) hot water. Cover and set aside for 12 minutes. Drain, discarding soaking water, and rinse under cold running water until the water runs clear.

Substitute an equal amount of green bell pepper for the red bell pepper.

A chard or collard leaf has a long, thick vein running through its center. When working with these greens, keep the soft vein at the top of the leaf intact. As you move toward the bottom (stem end) of the leaf, the vein becomes larger and tougher and needs to be removed. Lay the leaf flat on a cutting board and use a paring knife to remove the thick part of the vein and discard.

1 cup	whole raw cashews, soaked (see Tips, left)	250 mL
¼ cup	filtered water	60 mL
½ cup	chopped red bell pepper (see Tips, left)	125 mL
3 tbsp	nutritional yeast	45 mL
¼ tsp	fine sea salt	1 mL
⅛ tsp	turmeric	0.5 mL
2	large collard leaves (see Tips, left)	2

1. In a food processor fitted with the metal blade, process soaked cashews, water, red pepper, nutritional yeast, salt and turmeric until smooth, stopping motor once and scraping down sides of work bowl. Set aside.

2. Place collard leaves on a flat surface. Using a paring knife, remove the long vein from the center of each leaf so it is pliable.

3. Divide filling into 2 equal portions. Place one portion on uncut end of one leaf and roll up until you reach middle of the leaf. Fold over sides of leaf and continue rolling into a tight cylindrical package. Repeat with other leaf. Serve immediately or cover and refrigerate for up to 2 days.

Variation

Southwest Cashew Scramble Wrap: Add ¼ cup (60 mL) Mexican Fiesta Dressing (page 27) to each collard leaf along with the cashew mixture in Step 3.

Lemon Vanilla Cashew Yogurt

This "yogurt" reminds me of the creamy dairy product I loved as a kid. Try it on Chocolate Berry Pudding (page 35) or over a pile of fresh berries.

Makes
¾ cup (175 mL)

Tips

To soak the cashews, place in a bowl with 2 cups (500 mL) hot water. Cover and set aside for 12 minutes. Drain, discard soaking water and rinse under cold running water until water runs clear.

To get the maximum yield from citrus fruits, allow them to sit at room temperature for 30 minutes before juicing, then use the palm of your hand to roll it on the counter to release the juices.

½ cup	whole raw cashews, soaked (see Tips, left)	125 mL
¼ cup	filtered water	60 mL
2 tbsp	raw agave nectar	30 mL
1 tsp	finely grated lemon zest	5 mL
2 tbsp	freshly squeezed lemon juice (see Tips, left)	30 mL
¼ tsp	raw vanilla extract (see Tips, page 54)	1 mL

1. In a blender, combine soaked cashews, water, agave nectar, lemon zest and juice and vanilla. Blend at high speed until smooth. Transfer to a bowl. Serve immediately or cover and refrigerate for up to 4 days.

Variation

Chocolate Vanilla Cashew Yogurt: Substitute 2 tbsp (30 mL) raw cacao powder for the lemon zest and juice.

Orange Marmalade

This marmalade is a great addition to raw breakfast bowls. Try it stirred into Cinnamon Crunch Cereal (page 40), Almond Ginger Apple Hemp Cereal (page 39) or Breakfast Porridge (page 37), or spread it on Rise and Shine Bars (page 45).

Makes
2 cups (500 mL)

Tip

To soak the dates for this recipe, place in a bowl and add 2 cups (500 mL) hot water. Cover and set aside for 10 minutes. Drain, discarding soaking liquid.

2 tbsp	finely grated orange zest	30 mL
2 cups	chopped orange segments (see Tips, page 107)	500 mL
¾ cup	chopped pitted dates, soaked (see Tip, left)	175 mL

1. In a food processor fitted with the metal blade, process orange zest, orange segments and soaked dates until smooth. Transfer to a bowl. Serve immediately or cover and refrigerate for up to 3 days.

Variation

Orange Ginger Marmalade: Add ¼ cup (60 mL) chopped peeled gingerroot to the mixture.

Painted Fruit

Sweet, creamy tahini mixed with ripe berries and juicy pineapple makes a fresh breakfast that you will make time and time again.

Makes 1 serving

Tips

Tahini is a paste or butter made from ground sesame seeds that is similar to peanut or almond butter. Most store-bought tahini is made from sesame seeds that have been roasted, depriving it of its raw status. If you are following a strictly raw diet, be sure to look for products labeled "raw." If you have concerns, ask your purveyor.

When purchasing agave nectar, be sure to look for products labeled "raw." Most of the agave nectar on the market has been heated to a high temperature and so does not qualify as raw food. If you have concerns, ask your purveyor.

½ cup	raw tahini (see Tips, left)	125 mL
⅓ cup	filtered water	75 mL
3 tbsp	raw agave nectar (see Tips, left)	45 mL
2 cups	chopped hulled strawberries, divided	500 mL
1 cup	blueberries	250 mL
1 cup	chopped pineapple	250 mL

1. In a blender, combine tahini, water, agave nectar and 1 cup (250 mL) strawberries. Blend at high speed until smooth.
2. In a bowl, combine remaining strawberries, blueberries and pineapple with tahini cream. Mix well. Serve immediately or cover and refrigerate for up to 2 days.

Variations

For a creamier dish, substitute an equal amount of fresh Nut Milk (page 19) for the water.

Substitute an equal quantity of blueberries, chopped pineapple or chopped apple for the strawberries in Step 1.

I like to add ½ tsp (2 mL) raw vanilla extract in Step 1 and garnish with ¼ cup (60 mL) whole raw cashews and 2 to 3 tbsp (30 to 45 mL) raw shelled hemp seeds.

Try mixing other fresh fruit with the tahini cream in Step 2. Chopped apples, grapefruit, oranges, peaches, pears and nectarines all work well.

Spirulina-Painted Fruit: Substitute 1 tsp (5 mL) spirulina powder for the strawberries in Step 1.

Chocolate-Painted Fruit: Substitute 3 tbsp (45 mL) raw cacao powder for the strawberries in Step 1.

Smoothies, Drinks and Juices

continued on next page

Smoothies, Drinks and Juices *(continued)*

Water is fundamental to human life — our cells consist mostly of water. So it's not surprising that water plays a significant role in a successful raw food diet. Not only do we drink water but fruits and vegetables contain water, and it is their liquid component that enables us to easily transform these foods into refreshing and nutritious drinks.

Smoothies, freshly made juices and other drinks made from nutritious whole foods are one way to consume the nutrients you need to keep healthy. Drinking smoothies is one of the tricks for getting more raw, unprocessed foods into your diet. Smoothies, which are made in a blender, are quick and easy to prepare. They can combine ingredients such as dairy-alternative milks, leafy greens and fresh or frozen berries that you're likely to have on hand.

When making smoothies, you start with a liquid base such as a nut milk, fruit juice or water. Typical fruit and vegetable ingredients include berries, apples, pears, kale and celery. Nutritional balance is easily achieved by including ingredients such as hemp or flax seeds, or a spoonful or so of a nut or seed butter, which adds healthy fats and protein to the drink and also helps to create a creamy texture. To sweeten smoothies, add one or two pitted dates and/or some banana. Not only do these fruits add body, they provide added nutrients, including fiber. In fact, smoothies are distinguished from juices precisely because they contain fiber. Just be aware that fiber can make the drink very thick if you don't add enough liquid.

Because they do not contain fiber, juices are an extremely concentrated source of vitamins, minerals and phytonutrients. The absence of fiber means that your body can assimilate the nutrients more quickly. When you drink freshly made juices, your body doesn't need to burn energy to digest fiber, so it has time to relax, detoxifying and cleansing itself.

From fruit-based smoothies to vegetable-based juices, this chapter is full of fresh options. I love a tall glass of Everyone's Green Juice (page 90) first thing in the morning or Grapey Pear Juice (page 78) as a mid-afternoon pick-me-up. When I am famished and looking for something more substantial, I reach for a Kiwi Coconut Lime Smoothie (page 60) or a Garden Veggie Smoothie (page 70). Whether you prefer the sweet taste of fresh berries or the tart zing of lemon juice, you'll find a drink to satisfy every craving.

Blueberry Banana Cream Smoothie

The simplicity of this smoothie highlights the natural flavors of the berries and bananas. It's a wonderful summertime treat when blueberries are in season.

**Makes
2 cups (500 mL)**

Tips

Most flavoring extracts are not raw. Check the labels or contact purveyors if you have concerns. However, in raw food cuisine most organic extracts are acceptable, even those that have been distilled with steam.

To boost the protein content of your smoothie, try adding a scoop of your favorite protein powder — I prefer hemp or sprouted brown rice protein. Both are available in natural foods stores and well-stocked supermarkets. Not all are raw, though, so be sure to read the labels.

1 cup	Nut Milk (page 19; see Tips, page 53)	250 mL
2	bananas	2
½ cup	blueberries	125 mL
2 tbsp	melted coconut oil (see Tips, page 53)	30 mL
Dash	raw vanilla extract (see Tips, left)	Dash

1. In a blender, combine nut milk, bananas, blueberries, coconut oil and vanilla. Blend at high speed until smooth. Serve immediately.

Variation

Strawberry Cinnamon Banana Cream Smoothie: Substitute ½ cup (125 mL) hulled strawberries for the blueberries and a pinch of ground cinnamon for the vanilla.

Strawberry Cheesecake Smoothie

This smoothie is so sinfully sweet you won't believe it's good for you. The blend of rich cashews, aromatic vanilla and sweet strawberries is a match made in heaven.

Makes 1½ cups (375 mL)

Tips

You can substitute hemp milk for the Nut Milk (page 19).

To soak the cashews, place in a bowl and cover with warm water. Cover and set aside for 10 minutes. Drain, discarding soaking water.

Coconut oil is solid at room temperature. It has a melting temperature of 76°F (24°C), so it is easy to liquefy. To melt it, place in a shallow glass bowl over a pot of simmering water.

1 cup	Nut Milk (page 19; see Tips, left)	250 mL
½ cup	hulled strawberries	125 mL
⅓ cup	whole raw cashews, soaked (see Tips, left)	75 mL
2 tbsp	melted coconut oil (see Tips, left)	30 mL
½ tsp	raw vanilla extract	2 mL

1. In a blender, combine nut milk, strawberries, soaked cashews, coconut oil and vanilla. Blend until smooth. Serve immediately.

Variations

Mixed Berry Cheesecake Smoothie: Substitute ¼ cup (60 mL) blueberries, 3 to 4 raspberries and 2 to 3 blackberries for the strawberries.

If you prefer a sweeter smoothie, add 1 to 2 tbsp (15 to 30 mL) raw agave nectar.

Red Velvet Smoothie

A sweet and earthy blend of fresh beet juice and rich coconut butter, accented with aromatic vanilla, this smoothie is simply delicious.

¾ cup	filtered water	175 mL
¼ cup	fresh beet juice	60 mL
3 tbsp	coconut butter (see Tips, left)	45 mL
1 tbsp	raw cacao powder	15 mL
2 tsp	raw vanilla extract	10 mL
1	banana	1

Makes
1½ cups (375 mL)

1. In a blender, combine water, beet juice, coconut butter, cacao powder, vanilla and banana. Blend at high speed until smooth. Serve immediately.

Variation

For a creamier smoothie, substitute an equal amount of fresh Nut Milk or Hemp Milk (page 19) for the water.

Tips

Fresh beet juice can be used to color many different foods, such as cakes, muffins and pastries, or even clothing fibers such as cotton.

Coconut butter is a blend of coconut oil and coconut meat. You can usually find it in natural foods stores next to the coconut oil.

When purchasing raw vanilla extract, look for alcohol-free extract, to avoid the taste of raw alcohol in your smoothie.

Peachy Plum Smoothie

This smoothie is one of my all-time summer favorites. The unique flavors of juicy peaches and ripe plums are spiced up by a hint of cinnamon.

¾ cup	Nut Milk (page 19; see Tips, left)	175 mL
½ cup	sliced peach (see Tips, left)	125 mL
½ cup	sliced plums	125 mL
¼ tsp	ground cinnamon	1 mL
Dash	raw vanilla extract	Dash

Makes
1½ cups (375 mL)

1. In a blender, combine nut milk, peach, plums, cinnamon and vanilla. Blend at high speed until smooth. Serve immediately.

Tips

You can substitute Hemp Milk (page 19) for the Nut Milk.

To remove the stone from a peach, slice around the middle with a paring knife, cutting the fruit into two equal halves. If the peach is ripe, you can easily lift out the stone with your fingers.

Watermelon Peach Smoothie

This smoothie screams "summertime" with its blend of juicy, sweet peach and banana, refreshing watermelon and cooling mint.

1 cup	chopped seeded watermelon	250 mL
1/2 cup	sliced peach	125 mL
1	banana	1
2	chopped pitted dates (see Tips, page 61)	2
2 tbsp	fresh mint leaves	30 mL

**Makes
1 1/2 cups (375 mL)**

Tips

If your bananas ripen too quickly, remove the peels and store them in the freezer for the next time you want a cold, creamy smoothie.

To boost the protein content of your smoothie, try adding a scoop of your favorite protein powder — I prefer hemp or sprouted brown rice protein. Both are available in natural foods stores and well-stocked supermarkets. Not all are raw, though, so be sure to read the labels.

When stone fruits become ripe, store them in the refrigerator. This slows down the ripening process so they will keep for up to a week.

1. In a blender, combine watermelon, peach, banana, dates and mint. Blend at high speed until smooth. Serve immediately.

Variation

Frozen Blueberry Watermelon Peach Smoothie: Substitute 1/2 cup (125 mL) frozen blueberries for the banana and a pinch of ground cinnamon for the mint.

Mango Papaya Lime Smoothie

This smoothie is a tropical blend of juicy mango, ripe papaya and tart lime juice — perfect on warm-weather days.

**Makes
2 cups (500 mL)**

Tips

You can substitute Hemp Milk for the Nut Milk (page 19).

To peel and chop a mango, cut a small slice from the top and bottom of the fruit to make flat ends. Using a vegetable peeler, carefully peel away the skin. Stand the mango upright on a cutting board. Using a chef's knife, run the blade through the flesh, taking approximately three slices from each of the four sides. When you are close to the stone, use a paring knife to remove any remaining flesh from around the middle.

1 cup	Nut Milk (page 19; see Tips, left)	250 mL
½ cup	chopped peeled mango (see Tips, left)	125 mL
½ cup	chopped peeled papaya	125 mL
3 tbsp	freshly squeezed lime juice	45 mL
Dash	raw vanilla extract	Dash

1. In a blender, combine nut milk, mango, papaya, lime juice and vanilla. Blend at high speed until smooth. Serve immediately.

Variation

Substitute papaya with an equal amount of chopped cantaloupe or additional mango.

Melon Me Smoothie

Drink this sweet smoothie first thing in the morning. The fiber in the melon will keep you feeling full until lunch hour.

Makes
1½ cups (375 mL)

Tips

To ripen bananas quickly, place them in a paper bag with an uncut apple and tightly fold over the end of the bag. The apple will emit ethylene gas, which helps to speed ripening. Place the bag in a warm, dry area until the bananas are ripe.

To boost the protein content of your smoothie, try adding a scoop of your favorite protein powder — I prefer hemp or sprouted brown rice protein. Both are available in natural foods stores and well-stocked supermarkets. Not all are raw, though, so be sure to read the labels.

1 cup	chopped honeydew melon	250 mL
½ cup	chopped cantaloupe	125 mL
1	banana	1
1	pitted date, chopped (see Tips, page 61)	1
¼ cup	filtered water	60 mL
Dash	raw vanilla extract	Dash

1. In a blender, combine honeydew, cantaloupe, banana, date, water and vanilla. Blend at high speed until smooth. Serve immediately.

Melon Lime Smoothie

Juicy melon, fresh lime juice and tropical coconut oil make this a sweet, refreshing — and nutritious — smoothie for warm summer days.

1 cup	Nut Milk (page 19)	250 mL
½ cup	chopped honeydew melon	125 mL
3 tbsp	freshly squeezed lime juice	45 mL
2 tbsp	melted coconut oil (see Tips, left)	30 mL
¼ tsp	raw vanilla extract	1 mL

**Makes
2 cups (500 mL)**

Tips

Coconut oil is solid at room temperature. It has a melting temperature of 76°F (24°C), so it is easy to liquefy. To melt it, place in a shallow glass bowl over a pot of simmering water.

To boost the protein content of your smoothie, try adding a scoop of your favorite protein powder — I prefer hemp or sprouted brown rice protein. Both are available in natural foods stores and well-stocked supermarkets. Not all are raw, though, so be sure to read the labels.

1. In a blender, combine nut milk, melon, lime juice, coconut oil and vanilla. Blend at high speed until smooth. Serve immediately.

Variations

If you prefer a sweeter smoothie, add 1 to 2 tbsp (15 to 30 mL) raw agave nectar, to taste.

Substitute an equal amount of cantaloupe for the honeydew melon and 1 tbsp (15 mL) coconut butter for the coconut oil.

Citrus Explosion Smoothie

This tart and refreshing smoothie is a perfect way to start your day. Enjoy it with Rise and Shine Bars (page 45) or Breakfast Porridge (page 37).

**Makes
1¼ cups (300 mL)**

Tips

For a creamier smoothie, substitute an equal amount of fresh Nut Milk or Hemp Milk (page 19) for the water.

To yield the maximum juice from citrus fruits, allow them to sit at room temperature for 30 minutes before juicing. Once the fruit is at room temperature, use the palm of your hand to roll it on the counter to release the juices before slicing and squeezing.

Single-serve blenders with travel lids make it easy to take a smoothie with you on the go or to pack for travel. Check your local home or kitchen supply store for these handy appliances.

½ cup	filtered water (see Tips, left)	125 mL
1	banana	1
¼ cup	freshly squeezed orange juice (see Tips, left)	60 mL
3 tbsp	freshly squeezed lemon juice	45 mL
2 tbsp	freshly squeezed lime juice	30 mL

1. In a blender, combine water, banana and orange, lemon and lime juices. Blend at high speed until smooth. Serve immediately.

Variation

Substitute ¼ cup (60 mL) fresh grapefruit segments for the lime juice.

Kiwi Coconut Lime Smoothie

A creamy blend of tart citrus, sweet kiwifruit and rich coconut, this smoothie is a satisfying midday pick-me-up for when you are feeling peckish.

Makes
1½ cups (375 mL)

Tips

You can substitute Hemp Milk (see page 19) for the Nut Milk.

Use kiwifruit that are soft and ripe. To extract the flesh from kiwis, use a paring knife to remove a small amount of skin from the bottom. Carefully insert a small spoon (a grapefruit spoon is ideal) between the flesh and the skin and rotate it until the skin becomes loose. Scoop out the flesh.

Coconut oil is solid at room temperature but has a melting point of 76°F (24°C), so it is easy to liquefy. To melt it, place in a shallow glass bowl over a pot of simmering water.

1 cup	Nut Milk (page 19; see Tips, left)	250 mL
3	whole kiwifruit, peeled (see Tips, left)	3
1	banana	1
3 tbsp	freshly squeezed lime juice	45 mL
3 tbsp	melted coconut oil (see Tips, left)	45 mL

1. In a blender, combine nut milk, kiwi, banana, lime juice and coconut oil. Blend at high speed until smooth. Serve immediately.

Variation

To make this smoothie even creamier, substitute 2 tbsp (30 mL) coconut butter for the coconut oil.

Date Me Smoothie

Enjoy this creamy treat on its own as a snack or for breakfast, served with Cinnamon Crunch Cereal (page 40) or Painted Fruit (page 48).

**Makes
1½ cups (375 mL)**

Tips

If the dates you are using are hard, they may not blend easily. Prior to blending, place in a bowl with 2 cups (500 mL) hot water. Cover and set aside for 10 minutes to soften. Drain, discarding liquid.

There are numerous varieties of dates, but Medjool is my favorite. Although they are generally more expensive, Medjools are larger, softer and ideal for using in raw food recipes.

1 cup	Nut Milk (page 19)	250 mL
1	banana	1
6	chopped pitted dates (see Tips, left)	6
½ tsp	raw vanilla extract	2 mL
¼ tsp	ground cinnamon	1 mL

1. In a blender, combine nut milk, banana, dates, vanilla and cinnamon. Blend at high speed until smooth. Serve immediately.

Variation

For a smoothie that is even more filling, add a scoop of your favorite protein powder.

Butter Me Ripple Smoothie

This creamy smoothie tastes just like the ice cream it's named after. Filling and delicious, the blend of rich dates, sweet agave nectar, aromatic cinnamon and creamy almond butter makes this the perfect breakfast for when you are on the go.

Makes
2 cups (500 mL)

Tips

You can substitute Hemp Milk for the Nut Milk (page 19).

To boost the protein content of your smoothie, try adding a scoop of your favorite protein powder — I prefer hemp or sprouted brown rice protein. Both are available in natural foods stores and well-stocked supermarkets. Not all are raw, though, so be sure to read the labels.

1½ cups	Nut Milk (page 19; see Tips, left)	375 mL
6	chopped pitted dates (see Tips, page 61)	6
¼ cup	raw almond butter	60 mL
2 tbsp	raw agave nectar	30 mL
¼ tsp	ground cinnamon	1 mL

1. In a blender, combine nut milk, dates, almond butter, agave nectar and cinnamon. Blend at high speed until smooth. Serve immediately.

Cinnamon Goji Cream Smoothie

This smoothie is a sinfully sweet blend of nutritious goji berries, tropical coconut and warming cinnamon. Enjoy it on cooler days when you are craving something rich and satisfying.

Makes
1½ cups (375 mL)

Tips

Goji berries are small red berries native to China and Tibet. They have a mildly sweet flavor and are great additions to smoothies. You can find them in natural foods stores and most well-stocked grocery stores.

Coconut oil is solid at room temperature. It has a melting temperature of 76°F (24°C), so it is easy to liquefy. To melt it, place in a shallow glass bowl over a pot of simmering water.

1 cup	Nut Milk (page 19; see Tips, page 62)	250 mL
1	banana	1
¼ cup	goji berries (see Tips, left)	60 mL
2 tbsp	melted coconut oil (see Tips, left)	30 mL
¼ tsp	ground cinnamon	1 mL

1. In a blender, combine nut milk, banana, goji berries, coconut oil and cinnamon. Blend at high speed until smooth. Serve immediately.

Variation

Chocolate Goji Cream Smoothie: Substitute 2 tbsp (30 mL) raw cacao powder for the cinnamon and add 1 to 2 tbsp (15 to 30 mL) raw agave nectar, depending on desired sweetness.

Spiced Apricot Smoothie

This smoothie is a sweet, delicate blend of soft apricots and freshly ground aromatic spices — perfect during the holiday season or simply when you are craving something more filling.

	Makes 1½ cups (375 mL)	

Tips

To soak the apricots, place in a shallow bowl and add 1 cup (250 mL) warm filtered water. Cover and set aside for 10 minutes. Drain, discarding soaking liquid. Rinse under running water until the water runs clear.

When purchasing dried apricots, make sure to look for ones that are darker in color. This means that they have not been treated with sulfites to preserve color. Read the label to be sure they are sulfite-free, or ask your purveyor if you have concerns.

Use high-quality organic cinnamon. You will get the freshest flavor by grinding whole cinnamon sticks in a spice grinder.

½ cup	filtered water	125 mL
½ cup	freshly squeezed orange juice	125 mL
1	banana	1
½ cup	dried apricots, soaked (see Tips, left)	125 mL
¼ tsp	ground cinnamon	1 mL
Pinch	ground cloves	Pinch

1. In a blender, combine water, orange juice, banana, apricots, cinnamon and cloves. Blend at high speed until smooth. Serve immediately.

Variation

Substitute an equal quantity of ground allspice for the cloves.

Tahini Tzatziki (page 28) and Sunflower Seed Hummus (page 29)

Date Muesli (page 44)

Red Velvet Smoothie (page 54) and Everyone's Green Juice (page 90)

Apple Coconut Chews (page 98) and Coconut Mango Bites (page 99)

Grapefruit, Mint and Arugula Salad (page 107)

Red Pepper, Snap Pea and Ginger Cashew Salad (page 117)

Shred-Me-Up Slaw (page 121)

Angel Hair Beets and Greens (page 146)

Carrot Pad Thai (page 150)

Mocha Smoothie

This morning drink is a delicious replacement for coffee. Its creamy texture and coffee aroma will have you believing that you are drinking the real thing.

**Makes
1½ cups (375 mL)**

Tips

You can substitute hemp milk for the nut milk (page 19).

Most flavoring extracts are not raw. Check the labels or contact purveyors if you have concerns. However, in raw food cuisine most organic extracts are acceptable, even those that have been distilled with steam.

To extend the shelf life of ground spices such as cinnamon, store in an airtight container away from direct light.

1 cup	Nut Milk (page 19) (see Tips, left)	250 mL
1	banana	1
1 tbsp	raw coffee extract (see Tips, left)	15 mL
¼ tsp	ground cinnamon (see Tips, left)	1 mL
Dash	raw vanilla extract (see Tips, left)	Dash

1. In a blender, combine nut milk, banana, coffee extract, cinnamon and vanilla. Blend at high speed until smooth. Serve immediately.

Choco Mint Chip Smoothie

This smoothie is a blend of cooling peppermint, rich cacao, aromatic vanilla and sweet banana. Serve it with Chocolate Berry Pudding (page 35) for a simple yet decadent breakfast.

Tips

The broken pieces of hulled cacao beans, cacao nibs are often referred to as nature's chocolate chips. They are available in natural foods stores and well-stocked grocery stores.

To boost the protein content of your smoothie, try adding a scoop of your favorite protein powder — I prefer hemp or sprouted brown rice protein. Both are available in natural foods stores and well-stocked supermarkets. Not all are raw, though, so be sure to read the labels.

1 cup	Nut Milk (page 19)	250 mL
1	banana	1
¼ cup	raw cacao nibs (see Tips, left)	60 mL
½ tsp	raw mint extract (see Tips, page 65)	2 mL
¼ tsp	raw vanilla extract	1 mL

1. In a blender, combine nut milk, banana, cacao nibs, mint extract and vanilla. Blend at high speed until smooth. Serve immediately.

Variation

For a creamier smoothie, substitute 2 tbsp (30 mL) raw cacao powder for the cacao nibs.

Coconut Cutie Smoothie

Turn to this fresh and flavorful tropical smoothie to satisfy cravings for something sweet and rich.

Makes
1½ cups (375 mL)

Tips

You can substitute Hemp Milk for the Nut Milk (page 19).

Coconut butter is a blend of coconut oil and coconut meat. You can usually find it in natural foods stores next to the coconut oil.

Use unsweetened medium-shred unsulfured coconut. Not only is this type of coconut nutritionally beneficial, it also blends well in smoothies.

1 cup	Nut Milk (page 19; see Tips, left)	250 mL
1	banana	1
¼ cup	coconut butter (see Tips, left)	60 mL
2 tbsp	unsweetened dried shredded coconut (see Tips, left)	30 mL
½ tsp	raw vanilla extract (see Tips, page 65)	2 mL

1. In a blender, combine nut milk, banana, coconut butter, dried coconut and vanilla. Blend at high speed until smooth. Serve immediately.

Variation

Strawberry Coconut Cutie Smoothie: Add ½ cup (125 mL) chopped hulled strawberries.

Shamrock Shake

A delicious blend of fresh banana, sweet agave nectar, aromatic mint and nutrient-dense spirulina, this smoothie is perfect for breakfast on the go or as a midday pick-me-up.

**Makes
1½ cups (375 mL)**

Tips

You can substitute Hemp Milk for the Nut Milk (page 19).

Spirulina is a blue-green algae that has many healthful properties. It has trace amounts of vitamins and minerals and is a source of phytonutrients with anti-oxidant properties; it is also thought to be extremely detoxifying. Spirulina can be found in the supplements section of health food stores and in the natural foods section of well-stocked grocery stores.

1 cup	Nut Milk (page 19)	250 mL
1	banana	1
2 tbsp	raw agave nectar	30 mL
¼ tsp	spirulina powder (see Tips, left)	1 mL
Dash	raw mint extract	Dash

1. In a blender, combine nut milk, banana, agave nectar, spirulina and mint extract. Blend at high speed until smooth. Serve immediately.

Variation

To boost the nutritional value of this smoothie, add ¼ cup (60 mL) finely sliced kale.

V-5 Tomato Juice

This veggie cocktail is a flavorful mixture of ripe tomatoes, juicy cucumber, savory green pepper, fresh parsley and sweet carrots. Enjoy this with Tomato, Parsley and Onion Salad (page 110) or Creamy Cherry Tomato Salad (page 111).

**·Makes
2 cups (500 mL)**

Tips

Choose tomatoes for this juice that are still firm (not completely ripe); the juicer can extract more liquid from them. If your tomatoes are soft, place them in a blender along with 1/4 cup (60 mL) filtered water and blend until smooth. Strain through a fine-mesh sieve or cheesecloth, discarding the pulp.

Carrots are extremely high in beta-carotene, a carotenoid that your body converts to vitamin A. Because smoking and drinking alcohol reduce the levels of beta-carotene in the blood, consuming adequate amounts of this nutrient is recommended if you consume alcohol on a regular basis and/or smoke tobacco.

I like to use flat-leaf (Italian) parsley for juicing, as I find it has the best flavor, but feel free to use the curly variety if that is all you have.

- **Juicer**

3	tomatoes, quartered, divided (see Tips, left)	3
2	carrots, sliced if necessary, divided (see Tips, left)	2
1/2	cucumber, sliced if necessary, divided	1/2
1	small green bell pepper, quartered, divided	1
1/2 cup	flat-leaf (Italian) parsley (about 1/4 bunch), leaves and stems, divided (see Tips, left)	125 mL

1. In juicer, process 4 pieces tomato and one-third each of the carrots, cucumber, green pepper and parsley. Repeat until all of the vegetables and parsley have been juiced. Whisk well and serve immediately.

Garden Veggie Smoothie

Most people think of smoothies as thick, sweet, fruit-based drinks. This savory smoothie made with fresh vegetables is an easy way to sneak a few servings of vegetables into your diet — and a great afternoon treat.

Makes 2 cups (500 mL)

Tips

The outer stalks of celery can be tough and fibrous. For best results, peel the stalk with a vegetable peeler and save the peel to make soups, sauces or stocks.

Parsley comes in two different varieties: flat-leaf (also called Italian parsley) and curly. Both are very good for you. Flat-leaf parsley has more flavor when it is left in a roughly chopped state.

To ensure that any grit is removed from your parsley before chopping, place it in a bowl, cover with cool water and set aside for 2 minutes. The dirt will sink to the bottom of the bowl. Lift out the parsley, rinse under running water and pat dry or use a salad spinner to remove all excess moisture.

To store leafy green vegetables for an extended period, first wash and drain, then wrap them in a damp cloth or paper towels and store in your refrigerator's crisper for up to 2 weeks.

2 cups	chopped tomatoes	500 mL
1/2 cup	chopped celery (see Tips, left)	125 mL
1/4 cup	chopped parsley leaves (see Tips, left)	60 mL
1/4 cup	baby spinach	60 mL
2 tsp	freshly squeezed lemon juice	10 mL

1. In a blender, combine tomatoes, celery, parsley, spinach and lemon juice. Blend at high speed until smooth. Serve immediately.

Tomato Spinach Basil Smoothie

This smoothie is a perfect blend of ripe tomatoes and baby spinach, with a hint of fresh basil. For the best flavor, use high-quality extra virgin olive oil.

Makes **1½ cups (375 mL)**		

Tips

For this recipe, use tomatoes that are not only ripe but have a higher water content. Roma tomatoes will work if they are all that is available, but you may need to add ¼ cup (60 mL) filtered water to thin out the smoothie.

Always use a very sharp knife when cutting tomatoes, and remove the core before chopping. Insert the tip of a paring knife into the stem end and turn the tomato while holding the knife steady. Remove and discard the core.

Whenever you measure fresh herbs such as basil, make sure to press them firmly into the measuring cup to ensure exact measurement.

Although extra virgin olive oil should, by definition, be cold-pressed, it is worth checking the label. Some olive oils are extracted using a centrifuge system, which spins the olives at a very high speed. This heats the olives and the resulting oil, depriving it of its raw status.

You may substitute 1 tbsp (15 mL) flax oil or 2 tbsp (30 mL) cold-pressed hemp oil or chia seed oil for the olive oil.

2 cups	chopped tomatoes (see Tips, left)	500 mL
1 cup	baby spinach	250 mL
½ cup	packed fresh basil leaves (see Tips, left)	125 mL
2 tbsp	cold-pressed (extra virgin) olive oil (see Tips, left)	30 mL
1 tbsp	wheat-free tamari	15 mL

1. In a blender, combine tomatoes, spinach, basil, olive oil and tamari. Blend at high speed. Serve immediately.

Apple Kale Grape Juice

This simple and refreshing green juice will please any palate. Juicy apple, fresh kale and sweet grapes are a wonderful — and healthy — flavor combination.

**Makes
2 cups (500 mL)**

Tips

I like to use green kale (also called curly kale) in my juices because of its high water content; feel free to use black kale (also called lacinato or dinosaur kale) if that is what you have.

If you prefer a sweeter juice, use a red apple, such as Gala or McIntosh. If you prefer a less-sweet juice, choose a green apple, such as Granny Smith or Mutsu.

- **Juicer**

¼	head kale, divided (see Tips, left)	¼
½	cucumber, sliced, divided	½
2	celery stalks, divided	2
1	apple, quartered, divided (see Tips, left)	1
½ cup	green grapes, divided	125 mL

1. In juicer, process half of each of the ingredients. Repeat. Whisk well and serve immediately.

Variation

For a boost of nutrition, add 1 cup (250 mL) fresh sprouts, such as sunflower or pea sprouts.

Cucumber Cooler Juice

This recipe is a refreshing combination of cooling cucumber and mint and sweet melon. Serve it at your next summer barbecue to help beat the heat.(It also makes an especially good cocktail mixed with some vodka.)

**Makes
2 cups (500 mL)**

Tips

Substitute an equal amount of cantaloupe for the honeydew melon.

To peel and seed melon such as honeydew or cantaloupe, use a sharp chef's knife to cut a small slice from the top and bottom of the melon to make flat ends. On a cutting board, stand the melon upright on its stem-side and carefully use the knife to cut just under the peel in a downward motion to remove the skin. Then cut the melon in half, vertically. Using a large spoon, remove the seeds and discard.

To extend the shelf life of fresh herbs such as mint, wrap them in a damp towel and store in the crisper drawer of your refrigerator.

- **Juicer**

2	cucumbers, sliced	2
½	honeydew melon, peeled and sliced (see Tips, left)	½
1	bunch fresh mint, stems removed (see Tips, left)	1

1. In juicer, process cucumber, melon and mint. Whisk well and serve immediately.

Citrus Pineapple Carrot Juice

This juice is bursting with fresh, bold flavors. The pairing of slightly tart citrus with sweet pineapple and carrot is a great pick-me-up on a warm summer's day.

**Makes
2 cups (500 mL)**

Tips

Studies show that grapefruit helps to prevent fat from accumulating in the abdominal region, a condition known as metabolic syndrome, which can be a precursor to diabetes.

Whole vegetables such as carrots can go through the juicer as long as they will fit through the feed tube. Make sure you don't jam the machine by trying to put too much through at one time, and always use the proper tool to push the food through.

- **Juicer**

1	grapefruit (see Tips, page 75)	1
1	orange	1
¼	pineapple (about 1 cup sliced pineapple, skin on)	¼
2	carrots, sliced if necessary (see Tips, left)	2

1. Cut the grapefruit and orange in half and juice using a manual citrus juicer.
2. In juicer, process pineapple and carrots. Combine with grapefruit and orange juice and whisk well. Serve immediately.

Variations

Substitute an equal amount of fresh papaya for the pineapple.

If you prefer a sweeter juice, omit the carrots and substitute 2 apples, quartered.

Rise and Shine Juice

This morning favorite is a delicious blend of mouth-watering tangerine, tart grapefruit, fresh ginger and sweet apple.

**Makes
2 cups (500 mL)**

Tips

I don't recommend using a juicer to juice grapefruit or tangerines because that quantity of pith would make the juice bitter.

You can substitute 1 orange for the tangerines.

If you prefer a sweeter juice, use a red apple such as Gala or McIntosh. If you prefer a less sweet juice, choose a green apple such as Granny Smith or Mutsu.

Tailor the amount of ginger to your taste: add from $\frac{1}{2}$ inch (1 cm) up to 2 inches (5 cm) gingerroot, as desired.

- **Juicer**

1	grapefruit (see Tips, left)	1
2 to 3	tangerines (see Tips, left)	2 to 3
1	apple, quartered (see Tips, left)	1
1	piece (1 inch/2.5 cm) gingerroot (see Tips, left)	1

1. Cut the grapefruit and tangerines in half and juice using a manual citrus juicer.
2. In juicer, process apple and ginger. Combine with citrus juices and whisk well. Serve immediately.

Watermelon, Grapefruit and Mint Juice

This juice is best served on a warm summer's day over some crushed ice in a tall glass. Sweet watermelon is a perfect match for the tart grapefruit and refreshing mint.

> **Makes**
> **1½ cups (375 mL)**

Tips

To prevent fine herbs from turning brown after chopping, ensure that your knife is as sharp as possible, to prevent bruising.

To slice the mint finely, remove the leaves from their stems and stack them on top of each other. Roll the leaves into a cylinder and, using a sharp chef's knife, slice the cylinder into thin strips.

4 cups	chopped watermelon	1 L
½ cup	grapefruit juice	125 mL
3 tbsp	finely sliced fresh mint leaves, divided (see Tips, left)	45 mL

1. In a blender, combine watermelon, grapefruit juice and 2 tbsp (30 mL) sliced mint. Blend at high speed until smooth. Transfer to a glass and add the remaining mint. Whisk well and serve immediately.

Variation

Frozen Watermelon, Grapefruit and Blueberry Slush: Use frozen watermelon and add ½ cup (125 mL) frozen blueberries.

Apple Pear Lemonade

When I was a kid, I loved lemonade. As an adult I avoid most commercial brands because refined sugars have been added. This is a simple way to make fresh lemonade sweetened only with fruit.

**Makes
2½ cups (625 mL)**

Tips

Typically a medium-sized lemon will yield about 3 tbsp (45 mL) fresh lemon juice.

To yield the maximum juice from citrus fruits, allow them to sit at room temperature for 30 minutes before juicing. Once the fruit is at room temperature, use the palm of your hand to roll it on the counter to release the juices before slicing and squeezing.

- **Juicer**

2	apples, quartered	2
2	pears, quartered	2
½ cup	freshly squeezed lemon juice (see Tips, left)	125 mL
¼ cup	filtered water	60 mL
Pinch	ground cinnamon	Pinch

1. In juicer, process apples and pears.
2. Transfer resulting juice to a container and whisk in lemon juice, water and cinnamon. Serve immediately or cover and refrigerate for up to 2 days.

Grapey Pear Juice

This juice reminds me of the grape juice I used to drink as a kid. Most people don't ever think to juice whole grapes, but they yield a delicious drink.

Makes
1½ cups (375 mL)

Tip

Grapes are likely to contain high amounts of pesticides and herbicides (see page 10). When purchasing, buy organic grapes if possible.

- **Juicer**

2 cups	red grapes, divided (see Tips, left)	500 mL
2	pears, quartered, divided	2

1. In juicer, process ¼ cup (60 mL) grapes and 1 pear quarter. Repeat until all the grapes and pears have been juiced. Whisk and serve immediately.

Variation

Grapey Apple Juice: Substitute an equal quantity of white grapes for the red grapes and apples for the pears.

Carrot Pineapple Lemon Ginger Juice

I find that the natural sugars in this juice are a perfect remedy for when I'm craving something sweet and satisfying.

**Makes
1½ cups (375 mL)**

Tips

To peel and core a pineapple, place it on a cutting board and, using a sharp knife, cut off the top and bottom to remove the leaves and stem and create flat surfaces. This will reveal the thickness of the skin. Rest the pineapple on a flat end and, with a downward motion, slide the knife under the skin to remove the peel in strips. Shave off any remaining bits of peel with the knife. Cut the pineapple in half, then in quarters. Lay the quarters flat on a cutting board and, with the knife held at an angle, remove the core from each piece.

You may substitute 2 cups (500 mL) chopped fresh pineapple for the sliced pineapple.

- **Juicer**

4	medium carrots, sliced	4
¼	large pineapple, peeled, cored and sliced (see Tips, left)	¼
½	lemon, skin on, sliced	½
1	piece (1 inch/2.5 cm) gingerroot, skin on	1

1. In juicer, process carrots, pineapple, lemon and ginger. Whisk well and serve immediately.

Variation

Substitute an equal amount of lime for the lemon.

Apple Ginger Orange Juice

This unique blend of sweet apple and orange with a touch of savory ginger is high in vitamin C.

Makes
1¹⁄₂ cups (375 mL)

Tips

For a sweeter juice, use Gala, McIntosh, Ambrosia or Braeburn apples. For a less sweet version, try Red Delicious or Granny Smith apples.

If you prefer pulp-free juice, pour it through a fine-mesh sieve.

- **Juicer**

2	apples, quartered (see Tips, left)	2
2	pieces (1 inch/2.5 cm) gingerroot, skin on	2
¹⁄₂ cup	freshly squeezed orange juice	125 mL

1. In juicer, process apples and ginger. Transfer to a glass and add orange juice. Whisk well and serve immediately.

Lime Me Mon Juice

The mixture of tangy lime, sweet apple and fresh ginger makes this juice a perfect treat to satisfy those cravings for something sweet, whenever they hit.

**Makes
2 cups (500 mL)**

Tips

If you prefer a sweeter juice, use a red apple such as Gala or McIntosh. If you prefer a less sweet juice, choose a green apple such as Granny Smith or Mutsu.

To get the maximum yield from citrus, allow the fruit to sit at room temperature for 30 minutes before juicing. Once it is at room temperature, use the palm of your hand to roll it on the counter to release the juices before slicing and squeezing.

• **Juicer**

2	apples, quartered (see Tips, left)	2
1	pear, quartered	1
1	piece (1 inch/2.5 cm) gingerroot, skin on	1
6	limes (see Tips, left)	6

1. In juicer, process apples, pear and ginger.
2. Cut the limes in half and juice using a manual citrus juicer. Combine with apple, pear and ginger juice and whisk well. Serve immediately.

Variation

Lime Me Coconutty: Omit the apples in Step 1. In Step 2, combine 1 cup (250 mL) fresh coconut water with the lime, pear and ginger juice and whisk well. Transfer to a blender and add 2 tbsp (30 mL) coconut butter; blend until smooth. Serve immediately.

Sweet Lime Coconut Ginger Drink

This creamy drink is a flavorful blend of rich coconut, tart lime and spicy ginger. Enjoy it when it is cool outside — it will remind you of the tropics.

....

Makes
1½ cups (375 mL)

Tips

Coconut oil is solid at room temperature but has a melting point of 76°F (24°C), so it is easy to liquefy. To melt it, place in a shallow glass bowl over a pot of simmering water.

Coconut butter is a blend of coconut oil and coconut meat. You can usually find it in natural foods stores next to the coconut oil.

To remove the skin from gingerroot with the least amount of waste, use the edge of a teaspoon. With a brushing motion, scrape off the skin to reveal the yellow root.

¾ cup	filtered water	175 mL
¼ cup	freshly squeezed lime juice	60 mL
¼ cup	melted coconut oil (see Tips, left)	60 mL
2 tbsp	coconut butter (see Tips, left)	30 mL
2 tbsp	raw agave nectar	30 mL
2 tbsp	chopped peeled gingerroot (see Tips, left)	30 mL

1. In a blender, combine water, lime juice, coconut oil, coconut butter, agave nectar and ginger. Blend at high speed. Serve immediately.

Limey Cucumber Juice

A great mid-afternoon refreshment, this juice is a delicious blend of crisp cucumber, tart lime, sweet pear and aromatic celery.

**Makes
2 cups (500 mL)**

Tips

To get the maximum yield from citrus, allow the fruit to sit at room temperature for 30 minutes before juicing. Once it is at room temperature, use the palm of your hand to roll it on the counter to release the juices before slicing and squeezing.

I don't recommend using a juicer to juice the limes because that quantity of pith would make the juice bitter.

- **Juicer**

6	limes (see Tips, left)	6
1	cucumber, cut into 4 pieces	1
2	pears, quartered	2
4	stalks celery	4

1. Cut the limes in half and juice using a manual citrus juicer.
2. In juicer, process cucumber, pear and celery. Combine with lime juice and whisk well. Serve immediately.

Variation

For a sweeter spin on this juice, omit the pears and substitute 2 apples, quartered.

Gingery Tomato Juice

This recipe is one of my favorite ways to enjoy summer-fresh tomatoes at the peak of their season.

**Makes
1½ cups (375 mL)**

Tips

If the tomatoes you are using are not ripe, add up to 2 tsp (10 mL) raw agave nectar. Unripened tomatoes are generally not as sweet, so adding sweetener can help balance the flavors. Start by adding 1 tsp (5 mL) agave nectar, taste and then add 1 tsp (5 mL) more if necessary.

Typically a medium-sized lemon will yield about 3 tbsp (45 mL) fresh lemon juice.

• **Fine-mesh sieve**

4 cups	chopped tomatoes (see Tips, left)	1 L
3 tbsp	chopped peeled gingerroot	45 mL
¼ cup	filtered water	60 mL
1 tbsp	freshly squeezed lemon juice	15 mL
¼ tsp	fine sea salt	1 mL

1. In a blender, combine tomatoes, ginger, water, lemon juice and salt. Blend at high speed until smooth.
2. Transfer to fine-mesh sieve and, using the back of a spoon, gently press the mixture through. Serve immediately or transfer to an airtight container and refrigerate for up to 2 days.

Variation

Gingery Tomatillo Juice: Substitute an equal amount of chopped tomatillos for the tomatoes and add 2 tbsp (30 mL) raw agave nectar.

Lemon, Beet, Celery and Fennel Juice

I love the anise flavor that fresh fennel lends to the sweet beets and celery in this juice.

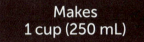

Makes
1 cup (250 mL)

Tips

Use a sharp chef's knife to cut the stalks off the fennel bulb. The stalks themselves are tough and have very little flavor. Reserve the soft green fronds for garnish and discard the stalks. You can store the fronds, submerged in water in an airtight container, in the refrigerator for up to 4 days.

When working with red beets, your hands can become stained by the juice. To prevent this, wear plastic gloves when handling them.

• **Juicer**

4	stalks celery, divided	4
1	bulb fennel, stalks removed, sliced, divided (see Tips, left)	1
1	large red beet, sliced, divided (see Tips, left)	1
¼	lemon, skin on	¼

1. In juicer, process 1 stalk celery, 1 slice fennel, 1 slice beet and lemon. Repeat with remaining celery, fennel and beet until all of the vegetables are juiced. Whisk and serve immediately.

Apple, Blueberry and Cabbage Juice

This sweet juice is best paired with a large salad, such as Fresh Herb Toss (page 105) or Lemony Wilted Kale and Beets (page 118).

**Makes
2 cups (500 mL)**

Tips

If you prefer a sweeter juice, use a red apple such as Gala or McIntosh. If you prefer a less sweet juice, choose a green apple such as Granny Smith or Mutsu.

When juicing cabbage, use the whole vegetable, including the core in the middle.

- **Juicer**

3	apples, quartered (see Tips, left)	3
2 cups	packed chopped purple cabbage (see Tips, left)	500 mL
2 cups	blueberries	500 mL
1/4 cup	filtered water	60 mL

1. In juicer, process apples and cabbage. Transfer to a glass and set aside.
2. In a blender, combine blueberries and water. Blend at high speed until smooth. Add to apple-cabbage juice and whisk well. Serve immediately.

Variation

Red Rover Juice: Substitute an equal amount of raspberries for the blueberries and 3 red beets, quartered, for the cabbage.

Apple, Beet and Cabbage Juice

This juice is a delicious pairing of sweet apple, rich beet and refreshing purple cabbage. Although it may sound odd, cabbage is actually quite sweet and refreshing when juiced.

**Makes
2 cups (500 mL)**

Tips

If you prefer a sweeter juice, use a red apple such as Gala or McIntosh. If you prefer a less sweet juice, choose a green apple such as Granny Smith or Mutsu.

Bunched beets are often accompanied by the beet greens, which are the leaves attached to fresh (not storage) beets. They are a fabulous dark green and can be juiced along with the beets.

- **Juicer**

4 cups	packed chopped purple cabbage	1 L
2	apples, quartered (see Tips, left)	2
1	medium red beet, quartered (see Tips, left)	1

1. In juicer, process cabbage, apples and beet. Whisk well and serve immediately.

Beet Me Green Juice

Vibrant red beets and beautiful fresh leafy greens give this juice its name. I like to enjoy it with Lemony Wilted Kale and Beets (page 118) for a simple lunch.

Makes **2 cups (500 mL)**		

Tips

Bunched beets include beet greens, which are the leaves attached to fresh (not storage) beets. They are a fabulous dark green vegetable that can be used in the same ways you use lettuce in salads.

When juicing vegetables that contain lower amounts of water, such as kale, follow them through the juicer with fruits or vegetables that are higher in water, such as celery. Sometimes the liquid from less juicy vegetables gets left in the gears of the juicer. Following them with a vegetable with high water content helps to flush it out.

- **Juicer**

3	large red beets, sliced, divided	3
4	collard green leaves, divided	4
1	bunch kale, divided	1
4	stalks celery, divided	4
1	apple, sliced, divided	1

1. In juicer, process a quarter of the beets, followed by 1 collard leaf, a quarter of the kale, 1 stalk celery and a quarter of the sliced apple. Repeat three times. Whisk and divide between two glasses, if desired.

Beta-Carotene Booster Juice

This rich blend of sweet carrots, apples and creamy sweet potatoes is so decadent you'll be tempted to drink it for dessert. Sweet potatoes are surprisingly easy to juice and help sweeten any mixture.

• •

**Makes
2 cups (500 mL)**

Tips

Carrots are extremely high in beta-carotene, a carotenoid that your body converts to vitamin A. Because smoking and drinking alcohol reduce the levels of beta-carotene in the blood, consuming adequate amounts of this nutrient is recommended if you consume alcohol on a regular basis and/or smoke tobacco.

Whole vegetables such as carrots can go through the juicer as long as they will fit through the feed tube. Make sure you don't jam the machine by trying to put too much through at one time, and always use the proper tool to push the food through.

If you prefer a sweeter juice, use a red apple such as Gala or McIntosh. If you prefer a less sweet juice, choose a green apple such as Granny Smith or Mutsu.

• **Juicer**

6	carrots, sliced (see Tips, left)	6
2	apples, quartered (see Tips, left)	2
1	medium sweet potato, sliced	1

1. In juicer, process carrots, apples and sweet potato. Whisk well and serve immediately.

Variation

Substitute an equal amount of peeled squash for the sweet potato.

Everyone's Green Juice

This juice is perfect for beginners looking to add green vegetables to their diet. The apples help to balance the bitterness of the dark leafy greens.

**Makes
2 cups (500 mL)**

Tip

The more often you consume bitter greens, the more your body will accept them. If you are just beginning to drink juices containing leafy greens, the addition of apple may make them easier to consume. Once you become accustomed to green juices, you can slowly decrease the quantity of apple and increase the quantity of bitter greens to suit your taste.

- **Juicer**

2	apples, quartered, divided	2
4	leaves romaine lettuce, divided	4
¼	bunch kale, divided	¼
½	cucumber, sliced, divided	½
2	celery stalks, divided	2

1. In juicer, process 2 apple quarters, 1 romaine leaf, a quarter of the kale, a quarter of the sliced cucumber and half a celery stalk. Repeat three times. Whisk and divide between two glasses, if desired.

Snacks

Snacking is important. Our blood sugar levels drop between major meals, so eating throughout the day helps to keep levels within the appropriate range — as long as you don't overdo it. Make sure that the treats you enjoy between meals are as healthy as the meals themselves. While potato chips may be tasty, they do nothing for your waistline and do not provide any real nutrition. Quite the contrary — they are usually loaded with refined salt and unhealthy fats.

Snacking on a raw food diet can be as simple as munching on an apple. But as satisfying as that can be, you want to be sure you are also eating protein and healthy fats. Sweet Vanilla Buckwheat Almond Clusters (page 97), Nori Pinwheels (page 96) and Pesto Crunch (page 94) are great to make ahead and take with you when you're on the go. Creamy Cashew Red Pepper Dip (page 95) is a tasty accompaniment to fresh carrot and celery sticks and a satisfying spread for crisp romaine leaves. Strawberry Hemp Cups (page 100) and Crunchy Chocolate Banana Pops (page 102) will let you indulge your sweet cravings.

This chapter contains snacks that are quick and easy to prepare. By combining a few simple ingredients, you will make delicious, nutritious treats that you can store in the refrigerator and enjoy all week long.

Teriyaki Almonds

I love the sweet-and-salty punch you get from these crunchy almonds. Make them to eat on the go or use them for a boost of protein, sprinkled over salads or Vegetable "Fried Rice" (page 165).

(page 165)

**Makes
2 cups (500 mL)**

Tips

While wheat-free tamari is not raw, it is gluten-free. The raw alternative for tamari, nama shoyu, does contain gluten. If you are following a completely raw diet and can tolerate gluten, by all means substitute an equal quantity of nama shoyu.

When purchasing nuts, be sure to look for products labeled "raw." Most nuts on the market have been roasted and do not qualify as raw food. If you have concerns, ask your purveyor.

If you are lucky enough to own an electric dehydrator, toss the almonds in the sauce and then place them in the dehydrator at 105°F (40°C) for 8 to 10 hours, or until all of the liquid has evaporated and the almonds are dry and slightly sticky. Cool completely. Store in an airtight container at room temperature for up to 14 days.

¼ cup	wheat-free tamari (see Tips, left)	60 mL
3 tbsp	raw agave nectar	45 mL
3 tbsp	sesame oil (untoasted)	45 mL
1 tbsp	chopped peeled gingerroot	15 mL
2 cups	whole raw almonds (see Tips, left)	500 mL

1. In a blender, combine tamari, agave nectar, sesame oil and ginger. Blend at high speed until smooth. Transfer to a bowl.

2. Add almonds and toss to combine. Serve immediately or cover and refrigerate for up to 7 days.

Variation

Teriyaki Cashews: Substitute an equal amount of cashews for the almonds.

Pesto Crunch

Nuts and seeds are a perfect grab-and-go snack solution when you have very little time. This mixture adds a fresh herb taste to a crunchy blend of almonds, cashews, sunflower seeds and pumpkin seeds.

Makes 4 servings

Tips

When purchasing nuts, be sure to look for products labeled "raw." Most nuts on the market have been roasted and do not qualify as raw food. If you have concerns, ask your purveyor.

Almonds are very nutritious. They include phytochemicals, protein, fiber and healthy fats, as well as vitamin E, magnesium, phosphorus, potassium, manganese and a small amount of B vitamins.

Cashews provide protein, copper, zinc, phosphorus, potassium and magnesium and are a source of healthy monounsaturated fat.

½ cup	whole raw almonds (see Tips, left)	125 mL
½ cup	whole raw cashews	125 mL
¼ cup	raw sunflower seeds	60 mL
¼ cup	raw pumpkin seeds	60 mL
½ cup	Green Pesto (page 26)	125 mL

1. In a bowl, combine almonds, cashews, sunflower seeds, pumpkin seeds and pesto. Toss until well coated. Serve immediately or cover and refrigerate for up to 3 days.

Variations

Substitute an equal amount of raw pine nuts or whole raw brazil nuts for the cashews and an equal amount of raw shelled hemp seeds for the sunflower seeds.

Southwest Crunch: Replace the Green Pesto with this spicy sauce. In a food processor fitted with the metal blade, combine 1 cup (250 mL) chopped red pepper, 2 tbsp (30 mL) freshly squeezed lemon juice, 2 tbsp (30 mL) filtered water, 2 tbsp (30 mL) wheat-free tamari, 1 tbsp (15 mL) chili powder and ¼ tsp (1 mL) cayenne pepper. Process until smooth. Toss the sauce with the nuts and seeds and serve immediately, or cover and refrigerate for up to 3 days.

Creamy Cashew Red Pepper Dip

Enjoy this creamy high-protein dip with fresh vegetables or some gluten-free crackers.

Makes
1½ cups (375 mL)

Tips

Typically a medium-sized lemon will yield about 3 tbsp (45 mL) fresh lemon juice.

To remove the skin from a clove of garlic, use the butt end of a chef's knife to press firmly but gently on the clove to loosen the skin. Using your index finger and thumb, carefully ease off the skin.

2 cups	whole raw cashews	500 mL
1 cup	chopped red bell pepper	250 mL
½ cup	chopped celery	125 mL
¼ cup	freshly squeezed lemon juice (see Tips, left)	60 mL
1 tsp	fine sea salt	5 mL
2	cloves garlic (see Tips, left)	2

1. In a food processor fitted with the metal blade, process cashews, red pepper, celery, lemon juice, salt and garlic until smooth, stopping motor to scrape down sides of work bowl as necessary. Transfer to a bowl. Serve immediately or cover and refrigerate for up to 4 days.

Variation

Creamy Walnut Red Pepper Dip: Substitute raw walnut halves for the cashews.

Nori Pinwheels

Working with raw nori sheets is easier than you might think. Make these delicious pinwheels ahead so you can enjoy them on busy days when you are on the go. For a complete meal, serve this with Fresh Herb Toss (page 105).

Makes 16 rolls

Tips

If you have a sushi mat, feel free to use it for this recipe.

Nori, a deep purple alga, and dulse, a red seaweed, are often referred to as "sea vegetables." They are among the best sources of natural iodine and also contain an appreciable amount of potassium. Iodine is essential for proper functioning of the thyroid gland, which produces hormones needed for growth, development, reproduction and a healthy metabolism.

To remove the skin from gingerroot with the least amount of waste, use the edge of a teaspoon. With a brushing motion, scrape off the skin to reveal the yellow root.

3	sheets raw nori, divided	3
1 cup	raw sunflower seeds	250 mL
½ cup	chopped celery	125 mL
¼ cup	filtered water	60 mL
¼ cup	freshly squeezed lemon juice	60 mL
1 tbsp	chopped peeled gingerroot (see Tips, left)	15 mL
½ tsp	fine sea salt	2 mL

1. In a food processor fitted with the metal blade, combine 1 sheet nori, sunflower seeds, celery, water, lemon juice, ginger and salt. Process until smooth, stopping motor to scrape down sides of work bowl as necessary. Transfer to a bowl.

2. Lay remaining nori sheets side by side on a flat surface. Divide sunflower seed mixture into two equal parts and spread evenly on each sheet. Starting at the bottom of the sheet, roll each up to form a cylinder (see Tips, left). Cut each roll into 8 equal pieces. Serve immediately or cover and refrigerate for up to 2 days.

Variation

Pumpkin Red Pepper Nori Pinwheels: Substitute pumpkin seeds for the sunflower seeds, chopped red bell pepper for the celery and 2 cloves garlic for the ginger.

Sweet Vanilla Buckwheat Almond Clusters

These sweet, crunchy and nutrient-dense clusters are the perfect midday pick-me-up.

Makes 7 clusters

Tips

Be sure to use raw buckwheat groats, not kasha, which has been toasted.

Two tablespoons (30 mL) chia seeds provide about 7 grams alpha-linolenic acid (ALA), an omega-3 fat that is an essential fatty acid — without it, we could not survive. It is called "essential" because our bodies are unable to make it and must obtain it from food. Good sources of ALA include flax seeds, chia seeds and walnuts.

- **Baking sheet lined with parchment**

½ cup	raw buckwheat groats (see Tips, left)	125 mL
2 tbsp	raw almond butter	30 mL
2 tbsp	raw agave nectar	30 mL
1 tbsp	raw chia seeds	15 mL
¼ tsp	raw vanilla extract	1 mL

1. In a bowl, combine buckwheat, almond butter, agave nectar, chia seeds and vanilla extract. Stir together until well incorporated. Using a tablespoon (15 mL), scoop up 7 equal portions and drop onto prepared baking sheet. Freeze for 15 minutes or until firm. Serve immediately or transfer to an airtight container and freeze for up to 2 weeks.

Variations

You can substitute an equal amount of raw cacao nibs, raw shelled hemp seeds or dried shredded coconut for the chia seeds.

Chocolate Buckwheat Almond Clusters: Substitute 1 tbsp (15 mL) raw cacao powder for the vanilla and 2 tsp (10 mL) raw cacao nibs for the chia seeds.

Nut-Free Vanilla Buckwheat Clusters: Substitute an equal amount of raw tahini for the almond butter.

Apple Coconut Chews

These sweet and rich cookie-like chews make a filling afternoon snack or a tasty after-dinner treat.

Makes 4 servings

Tips

Coconut butter is a blend of coconut oil and coconut meat. You can usually find it in natural foods stores next to the coconut oil.

I like to use Granny Smith apples in this recipe. Their tart flavor helps to balance the rich coconut and sweet agave nectar, but by all means use whatever apples you have on hand.

Use unsweetened medium-shred unsulfured coconut. Not only is this type of coconut nutritionally beneficial, the medium shred size will help the chews hold together.

- **Baking sheet lined with parchment**

¼ cup	raw agave nectar	60 mL
¼ cup	ground raw flax seeds	60 mL
½ cup	coconut butter (see Tips, left)	125 mL
1 cup	chopped apple (see Tips, left)	250 mL
1 cup	dried shredded coconut (see Tips, left)	250 mL

1. In a food processor fitted with the metal blade, process agave nectar, flax seeds and coconut butter until smooth, stopping motor to scrape down sides of work bowl as necessary. Add apple and coconut and pulse 4 to 6 times to combine.

2. Using a tablespoon (15 mL), scoop up 4 equal portions and drop onto prepared baking sheet. Freeze for 10 to 12 minutes or until firm enough to handle. Serve immediately or transfer to an airtight container and refrigerate for up to 2 days.

Variation

Add ¼ tsp (1 mL) raw vanilla extract in Step 1.

Coconut Mango Bites

Serve these sweet, rich bites with a fresh Peachy Plum Smoothie (page 54) or Spiced Apricot Smoothie (page 64).

. . . .

**Makes
12 to 15 bites**

Tips

To soak the mango, place in a bowl with 3 cups (750 mL) hot water. Cover and set aside for 13 minutes. Drain, discarding soaking water.

When purchasing dried fruits such as mango or apricots, be sure to look for products labeled "unsulfured." Sulfur dioxide is a chemical that is sometimes used on dried fruits to prevent oxidization and retain color.

Coconut oil is solid at room temperature but has a melting point of 76°F (24°C), so it is easy to liquefy. To melt it, place in a shallow glass bowl over a pot of simmering water.

2 cups	dried mango, soaked (see Tips, left)	500 mL
¼ cup	raw agave nectar	60 mL
1 cup	dried shredded coconut, divided (see Tips, page 98)	250 mL
¼ cup	melted coconut oil (see Tips, left)	60 mL
2 tsp	freshly grated lemon zest	10 mL

1. In a food processor fitted with the metal blade, process soaked mango, agave nectar, ¾ cup (175 mL) shredded coconut, coconut oil and lemon zest until well combined. Transfer to a bowl.
2. Using an ice-cream scoop or small ladle, divide mixture into 12 to 15 equal portions.
3. Place remaining ¼ cup (60 mL) shredded coconut in a shallow bowl. Using the palms of your hands, roll each portion of mixture into a ball, then roll each ball in shredded coconut until completely coated. Serve immediately or transfer to an airtight container and refrigerate for up to 7 days.

Variation

Coconut Apricot Bites: Substitute an equal amount of dried apricots for the dried mango and ½ tsp (2 mL) ground cinnamon for the lemon zest in Step 1.

Strawberry Hemp Cups

I love this snack when I am craving something sweet yet substantial. Hemp seeds make a perfect — and super-healthy — filling for juicy ripe strawberries.

Makes 2 servings

Tips

To soak the hemp seeds, place in a bowl and add 1 cup (250 mL) warm water. Cover and set aside for 10 minutes. Drain, discarding soaking liquid. Rinse under cold running water until the water runs clear.

To store hemp seeds, place them in an airtight container and refrigerate; this will prevent the fats from turning rancid. Hemp seeds can also be frozen for up to 6 months. They are extremely high in protein, containing up to 5 grams per tablespoon (15 mL).

To remove the core from a strawberry, insert the tip of a paring knife at a slight angle into the center of the top of the berry. Rotate the strawberry around the tip of the knife to expose the core. Remove and discard.

½ cup	hemp seeds, soaked (see Tips, left)	125 mL
¼ cup	filtered water	60 mL
3 tbsp	raw agave nectar	45 mL
1 tbsp	freshly squeezed lemon juice	15 mL
Dash	raw vanilla extract	Dash
1 cup	strawberries, hulled (see Tips, left)	250 mL

1. In a blender, combine soaked hemp seeds, water, agave nectar, lemon juice and vanilla. Blend at high speed until smooth. Transfer to a bowl.

2. Using a teaspoon (5 mL), carefully stuff each strawberry with the hemp filling. Transfer to a serving plate. Serve immediately or cover and refrigerate for up to 3 days.

Cinnamon Apple Almond Stacks

Crisp fresh apples, crunchy almonds and aromatic cinnamon — all snacks should be this delicious!

Makes 2 servings

Tips

Almonds are very nutritious. They include phytochemicals, protein, fiber and healthy fats, as well as vitamin E, magnesium, phosphorus, potassium, manganese and a small amount of B vitamins.

Use high-quality organic cinnamon. You will get the freshest flavor by grinding whole cinnamon sticks in a spice grinder.

To remove the apple cores, slice the fruits in half lengthwise. Using a melon baller or a teaspoon, scoop out the seeds and tough core.

½ cup	whole raw almonds	125 mL
½ tsp	ground cinnamon (see Tips, left)	2 mL
2	apples, unpeeled, cored (see Tips, left)	2
3 tbsp	raw agave nectar	45 mL
¼ cup	raw almond butter	60 mL

1. In a food processor fitted with the metal blade, process almonds and cinnamon until nuts are roughly chopped (you want to retain some texture). Transfer to a shallow bowl.

2. Using a sharp paring knife, cut apples crosswise into slices ¼ inch (0.5 cm) thick (depending on size of apples, this should yield 3 or 4 thick slices per apple). Lay apple slices on a flat surface and drizzle with half the agave nectar. Flip slices over and repeat. Using your fingers, gently press both sides of apple slices in almond mixture until evenly coated.

3. Gently spread each slice of nut-coated apple with about 1 tsp (5 mL) almond butter. Stack slices on top of one another, roughly reassembling the apples to make two equal portions. Transfer to a serving plate and enjoy immediately.

Variations

Substitute pears for the apples.

Substitute raw pumpkin seed butter for the almond butter.

Crunchy Chocolate Banana Pops

Serve these crunchy sweet treats with a nice tall glass of Nut Milk (page 19) — it's a perfect afternoon snack.

Makes 4 pops

Tips

Coconut oil is solid at room temperature but has a melting point of 76°F (24°C), so it is easy to liquefy. To melt it, place in a shallow glass bowl over a pot of simmering water.

Cacao powder is powdered raw chocolate. It is similar to cocoa powder but tastes even better, with a deeper, richer flavor. Cacao powder is available in well-stocked supermarkets and natural foods stores and online. If you are transitioning to a raw food diet and can't find it, you may substitute an equal quantity of good-quality cocoa powder, but note that the beans in cocoa powder have been roasted, depriving them of their raw status. If you are following a strictly raw diet, use cacao powder.

- **Baking sheet lined with parchment**

¼ cup	melted coconut oil (see Tips, left)	60 mL
¼ cup	filtered water	60 mL
3 tbsp	raw cacao powder (see Tips, left)	45 mL
3 tbsp	raw agave nectar	45 mL
4	bananas, peeled	4

1. In a blender, combine coconut oil, water, cacao powder and agave nectar. Blend at high speed until smooth. Transfer mixture to a shallow dish large enough to accommodate the bananas.

2. Using your hands, dip each banana in mixture until evenly coated. Place on prepared baking sheet and freeze for 10 minutes or until coating has set and outside is firm enough to handle. Serve immediately or transfer to an airtight container and freeze for up to 5 days.

Variations

Substitute 12 to 16 apple slices, 12 to 15 strawberries or 6 organic dried pineapple rings for the banana.

Salads

When we hear the words "raw food," we almost automatically think of salad. While salads are an important part of a raw food diet, not just any salad will suffice. For instance, while you may enjoy a traditional salad of iceberg lettuce with tomato slices, cucumbers and French dressing, if that's all you are having for a meal you will not get all the nutrients you need to help sustain a busy lifestyle. You need a salad that's packed with a wide range of nutrients. Start with nourishing greens such as kale, arugula, spinach, bok choy, cabbage or chard. Then add ingredients that expand the range of nutrients provided, such as avocado, which is rich in healthy monounsaturated fats; carrots, which provide beta-carotene and other healthful carotenoids that your body converts to vitamin A; beets, which contain minerals such as magnesium; and hemp or pumpkin seeds, which add protein, along with other valuable nutrients, to name just a few. Not only will they help you to feel satiated, but by consistently including a wide variety of nutrient-dense ingredients in your diet, you will ensure that your body gets all the nutrients it needs.

Salads don't need to be complicated. These salad recipes use fresh, flavorful ingredients and are simple to prepare. Many of the recipes start with a base of raw vegetables such as broccoli, carrots or beets, thinly sliced, shredded or shaved. Salads such as Crunchy Asian Greens (page 116) and Lemony Wilted Kale and Beets (page 118) are a perfect midday meal. Others, such as Parsley Almond Tabouli (page 109) and Chunky Cucumber Corn Salad (page 113), rely on contrasting textures to provide a delicious outcome.

Once you understand how to build well-balanced salads using these recipes, you'll feel confident enough to create your own combinations. Turn to the Dressings chapter (page 125) for a range of tasty and nutritious dressings to drizzle on your creations. Lemon Tahini Dressing (page 131) and Coconut Garlic Dressing (page 136) are multipurpose dressings that can be used with virtually any salad. Others, such as Curried Carrot Dressing (page 135) and Berry Vinaigrette (page 140), are best paired with specific salads — in this case, Sweet Pepper Slaw (page 124) and Watermelon and Cashew Salad (page 108).

Whatever your tastes, in this chapter you'll find many easy-to-prepare salads that are not only delicious but will also help to satisfy your appetite, sustain your busy lifestyle and, I hope, inspire you to incorporate salads into your meals more often.

Fresh Herb Toss

Most people don't realize how nutritious and tasty soft green herbs can be in salads. In this dish their fresh, bold flavors take center stage.

Makes 2 side salads

Tips

The stalks of the leaves closest to the bottom of fresh cilantro stems are generally tough and need to be removed. Those on leaves closer to the top are softer and do not need to be removed.

To finely slice the basil, remove the leaves from the stems and stack them on top of each other. Roll the leaves into a cylinder and, using a sharp chef's knife, slice the cylinder into thin strips.

Flat-leaf parsley has much more flavor and is easier to chew than curly parsley.

2 cups	fresh cilantro leaves, large stems removed (see Tips, left)	500 mL
1 cup	finely sliced fresh basil leaves (see Tips, left)	250 mL
½ cup	fresh flat-leaf (Italian) parsley leaves	125 mL
3 tbsp	cold-pressed (extra virgin) olive oil	45 mL
2 tbsp	freshly squeezed lemon juice	30 mL
¼ tsp	fine sea salt	1 mL

1. In a bowl, combine cilantro, basil and parsley. Add olive oil, lemon juice and salt. Toss well. Serve immediately or cover and refrigerate for up to 2 days.

Citrus Mint Toss

This salad reminds me of Mediterranean dishes bursting with fresh green herbs and sweet citrus. Serve it with Vegetable "Fried Rice " (page 165) or Summer Corn Cakes (page 162).

**Makes
1 main-course or
2 side salads**

Tips

To finely slice the mint, remove the leaves from the stems and stack them on top of each other. Roll the leaves into a cylinder and, using a sharp chef's knife, slice the cylinder into thin strips.

I prefer to use organic sea salt. This type of salt is classified as a whole food and is said to contain many trace minerals. If salt intake is something you are concerned about, feel free to use less than called for or omit it completely.

½ cup	orange segments (see Tips, page 107)	125 mL
½ cup	grapefruit segments	125 mL
¼ cup	lemon segments (see Tips, page 107)	60 mL
1 cup	finely sliced mint leaves (see Tips, left)	250 mL
2 tbsp	cold-pressed (extra virgin) olive oil	30 mL
¼ tsp	fine sea salt	1 mL

1. In a bowl, combine orange, grapefruit and lemon segments and mint. Add olive oil and salt. Toss well. Serve immediately or transfer to an airtight container and refrigerate for up to 2 days.

Variation

Substitute an equal quantity of lime segments for the lemon.

Grapefruit, Mint and Arugula Salad

This salad is a delicious balance of slightly bitter grapefruit, fresh mint and peppery arugula. The grapefruit makes the addition of lemon juice or vinegar unnecessary.

**Makes
1 main-course or
2 side salads**

Tips

To prepare the citrus segments for this recipe, place on a cutting board and remove a bit of skin from each end to create a flat surface — this will reveal the thickness of the pith. Using a sharp knife in a downward motion, remove the skin and the pith. Shave off any remaining bits of pith, then cut between the membranes to produce wedges of pure citrus flesh.

To finely slice the mint, remove the leaves from the stems and stack them on top of each other. Roll the leaves into a cylinder and, using a sharp chef's knife, slice the cylinder into thin strips.

2 cups	baby arugula	500 mL
1 cup	grapefruit segments (about 1 small; see Tips, left)	250 mL
½ cup	finely sliced fresh mint leaves (see Tips, left)	125 mL
2 tbsp	cold-pressed (extra virgin) olive oil	30 mL
1 tbsp	raw agave nectar	15 mL

1. In a serving bowl, toss arugula, grapefruit, mint, olive oil and agave nectar until well combined. Serve immediately or cover and refrigerate for up to 1 day.

Variations

Orange, Mint and Arugula Salad: Substitute an equal quantity of orange segments for the grapefruit.

For a boost of protein, add 3 tbsp (45 mL) raw shelled hemp seeds. Hemp seeds contain all eight essential amino acids, which makes them a complete protein. One tablespoon (15 mL) hemp seeds contains up to 5 grams of complete protein.

Watermelon and Cashew Salad

Watermelon pairs beautifully with nuts, seeds and spices and is wonderfully refreshing on a warm summer's day. Enjoy this salad with a dollop of Quick Thai Cream Sauce (page 23) and some Belgian endive leaves for scooping.

**Makes
1 main-course or
2 side salads**

Tips

Cashews provide protein, copper, zinc, phosphorus, potassium and magnesium and are a source of healthy monounsaturated fat.

You may substitute 2 tbsp (30 mL) thinly sliced fresh oregano leaves for the dried oregano.

To boost the protein content of your smoothie, try adding a scoop of your favorite protein powder — I prefer hemp or sprouted brown rice protein. Both are available in natural foods stores and well-stocked supermarkets. Not all are raw, though, so be sure to read the labels.

½ cup	whole raw cashews	125 mL
1 tbsp	cold-pressed (extra virgin) olive oil	15 mL
1 tsp	dried oregano (see Tips, left)	5 mL
¼ tsp	fine sea salt	1 mL
2 cups	cubed seeded watermelon	500 mL
2 tbsp	finely sliced green onion (green part only)	30 mL

1. In a food processor fitted with the metal blade, process cashews until roughly chopped. Add olive oil, oregano and salt. Process until just combined, about 5 seconds, or until cashews just begin to stick together.

2. In a bowl, combine watermelon and green onion. Toss well. Using a fine-mesh sieve, drain off any excess liquid and discard. Add cashew mixture to watermelon and mix well. Serve immediately or cover and refrigerate for up to 2 days.

Parsley Almond Tabouli

This Mediterranean-inspired recipe is packed full of healthy protein and fiber. It's perfect as a midday snack or as a main course served with Carrot Pad Thai (page 150).

**Makes
1 main-course or
2 side salads**

Tips

You can substitute curly parsley for the flat-leaf parsley.

Almonds are very nutritious. They include phytochemicals, protein, fiber and healthy fats, as well as vitamin E, magnesium, phosphorus, potassium, manganese and a small amount of B vitamins.

Apple cider vinegar has long been used in folk medicine. It is a great digestive aid, among its other benefits. When purchasing apple cider vinegar, make sure that it is raw, was made from organically grown apples and contains the "mother," which is a source of healthy bacteria and enzymes.

2 cups	roughly chopped flat-leaf (Italian) parsley leaves (see Tips, left)	500 mL
½ cup	whole raw almonds	125 mL
½ cup	finely chopped seeded red bell pepper	125 mL
3 tbsp	raw (unpasteurized) apple cider vinegar (see Tips, left)	45 mL
2 tbsp	cold-pressed (extra virgin) olive oil	30 mL
½ tsp	fine sea salt	2 mL

1. In a food processor fitted with the metal blade, process parsley and almonds until roughly chopped and no large pieces remain, about 10 seconds.
2. Transfer to a bowl. Stir in red pepper, vinegar, olive oil and salt. Toss well. Serve immediately or transfer to an airtight container and refrigerate for up to 2 days.

Tomato, Parsley and Onion Salad

I love the way Italian cuisine marries bold flavors by using fresh produce. This salad is simple, fresh and delicious.

· ·

Makes 1 main-course or 2 side salads		

Tips

If you can, use heirloom tomatoes for this salad. Heirloom tomatoes have a meatier texture and are more flavorful than most commercial tomatoes. Look for varieties such as Green Zebra, Oaxacan Jewel, Brandywine and Purple Russian. Check out your local farmers' market to see what is available.

Store unripened tomatoes at room temperature, away from direct light. Once they have ripened, serve them immediately or refrigerate until ready to use.

1 cup	chopped tomatoes (see Tips, left)	250 mL
½ cup	roughly chopped flat-leaf (Italian) parsley leaves	125 mL
¼ cup	finely sliced red onion	60 mL
3 tbsp	cold-pressed (extra virgin) olive oil	45 mL
2 tbsp	raw (unpasteurized) apple cider vinegar (see Tips, page 109)	30 mL
¼ tsp	fine sea salt	1 mL

1. In a bowl, combine tomatoes, parsley and onion. Add olive oil, vinegar and salt. Toss until well combined. Serve immediately or cover and refrigerate for up to 1 day.

Creamy Cherry Tomato Salad

Add some healthy fat to your diet with this salad, which combines the sweet, juicy pop of cherry tomatoes with smooth, creamy avocado.

**Makes
2 main-course or
4 side salads**

Tips

To ripen avocados, place them in a brown paper bag with a tomato or an apple. If your avocado is ripe and won't be consumed within a day or two, place it in the coolest part of the refrigerator to lengthen its life by 3 to 4 days. Once you take an avocado out of the fridge, do not put it back in — it will turn black.

You can substitute 1/4 cup (60 mL) fresh basil leaves for the dried basil.

2	medium avocados, divided (see Tips, left)	2
1/4 cup	freshly squeezed lemon juice	60 mL
2 tbsp	cold-pressed (extra virgin) olive oil	30 mL
1/4 cup	filtered water	60 mL
1 tbsp	dried basil (see Tips, left)	15 mL
1/2 tsp	fine sea salt	2 mL
2 cups	halved cherry tomatoes	500 mL

1. In a food processor fitted with the metal blade, combine 1 avocado, lemon juice, olive oil, water, basil and salt. Process until smooth.
2. Cut the remaining avocado into 1-inch (2.5 cm) cubes and place in a bowl. Add tomatoes and avocado purée. Toss well to coat. Serve immediately or cover and refrigerate for up to 1 day.

Caprese Stacked Salad

I love this simple take on the classic Italian favorite. The fat from the cashews is a wonderful stand-in for mozzarella cheese.

Makes 2 side salads

Tips

Heirloom tomatoes have a meatier texture and are more flavorful than most commercial tomatoes. Look for varieties such as Green Zebra, Oaxacan Jewel, Brandywine and Purple Russian. Check out your local farmers' market to see what is available.

To finely slice the basil, remove the leaves from the stems and stack them on top of each other. Roll the leaves into a cylinder and, using a sharp chef's knife, slice the cylinder into thin strips.

You can substitute 1/2 cup (125 mL) Green Pesto (page 26) for the sliced basil.

2	medium-sized tomatoes, cores removed (see Tips, left)	2
1 cup	whole raw cashews	250 mL
1/2 cup	filtered water	125 mL
1/4 cup	freshly squeezed lemon juice	60 mL
1/4 tsp	fine sea salt	1 mL
1/2 cup	finely sliced fresh basil leaves (see Tips, left)	125 mL

1. Using a sharp chef's knife, slice each tomato into 4 or 5 slices. Arrange slices in a single layer on a serving plate and set aside.
2. In a blender, combine cashews, water, lemon juice and salt. Blend at high speed until smooth.
3. Place a dollop of cashew purée on top of each tomato slice, followed by a generous amount of basil. Arrange tomato slices in two equal stacks. Serve immediately or transfer to an airtight container and refrigerate for up to 2 days.

Chunky Cucumber Corn Salad

Cucumbers give this salad a refreshing crunch. Serve this underneath Summer Corn Cakes (page 162) for a delectable treat.

**Makes
1 main-course or
2 side salads**

Tips

To prepare the cucumber for this recipe, use a sharp chef's knife to cut a piece from each end to create flat surfaces. Using a vegetable peeler, peel the cucumber. Cut the cucumber in half lengthwise and, using a spoon, scoop out and discard the seeds.

To remove kernels from a cob of corn, cut pieces from the top and bottom of the cob to create flat surfaces. Stand up the cob on a flat end. Using a chef's knife in a downward motion, gently strip away the kernels, making sure not to remove too much of the starchy white body of the cob.

2 cups	roughly chopped peeled, seeded cucumber (see Tips, left)	500 mL
1 cup	fresh corn kernels (see Tips, left)	250 mL
1/4 cup	chopped red bell pepper	60 mL
3 tbsp	cold-pressed (extra virgin) olive oil	45 mL
2 tbsp	freshly squeezed lemon juice	30 mL
1/4 tsp	fine sea salt	1 mL

1. In a bowl, combine cucumber, corn, red pepper, olive oil, lemon juice and salt. Toss until well combined. Serve immediately or cover and refrigerate for up to 2 days.

Sesame Ginger Sea Veggies

Not only are sea vegetables nutritious and easy to use, they are also versatile and quick to absorb flavor. Serve this salad with Sesame Garlic Dressing (page 136) and Lo Mein "Stir-Fry" (page 151).

Makes 1 main-course or 2 side salads

Tips

Arame is a nutritious sea vegetable. Most sea vegetables are sold in a dry state. To rehydrate them, simply cover in twice their volume of warm water and set aside for 15 minutes or until softened.

To remove the skin from gingerroot with the least amount of waste, use the edge of a teaspoon. With a brushing motion, scrape off the skin to reveal the yellow root.

¼ cup	dried arame (see Tips, left)	60 mL
1 cup	warm filtered water	250 mL
2	sheets nori, sliced thinly	2
¼ cup	finely sliced ginger (see Tips, left)	60 mL
3 tbsp	cold-pressed sesame oil (untoasted)	45 mL
2 tbsp	wheat-free tamari (see Tips, page 115)	30 mL

1. In a small bowl, combine arame and water. Cover and set aside for 15 minutes, until softened. Drain, discarding soaking liquid.
2. In a bowl, combine arame, nori, ginger, sesame oil and tamari. Toss until well combined. Serve immediately or cover and refrigerate for up to 3 days.

Variations

Substitute an equal amount of wakame for the arame.

Creamy Lemon Garlic Cucumber Sea Veggies: Substitute ½ cup (125 mL) Tahini Tzatziki (page 28) for the ginger, sesame oil and tamari in Step 2.

Crunchy Sesame Mushroom Salad

Umami is a Japanese word that means "delicious flavor" and is often used to describe savory foods. Marinating mushrooms in dark, rich tamari gives them umami and the mouth feel of cooked mushrooms. The sesame seeds in this salad provide not only a nice crunch but extra nutrition too.

**Makes
1 main-course or
2 side salads**

Tips

If the mushrooms are rather large, cut them into slices to suit.

While wheat-free tamari is not raw, it is gluten-free. The raw alternative for tamari, nama shoyu, does contain gluten. If you are following a completely raw diet and can tolerate gluten, by all means substitute an equal quantity of nama shoyu.

2 cups	button mushrooms, quartered (see Tips, left)	500 mL
¼ cup	cold-pressed sesame oil (untoasted)	60 mL
3 tbsp	wheat-free tamari (see Tips, left)	45 mL
¼ cup	raw sesame seeds	60 mL
1 tbsp	chopped fresh thyme leaves	15 mL

1. In a bowl, combine mushrooms, sesame oil, tamari, sesame seeds and thyme. Toss until well coated. Cover and set aside for 15 minutes, until softened. Serve immediately or cover and refrigerate for up to 3 days.

Variations

Substitute an equal amount of cold-pressed (extra virgin) olive oil for the sesame oil.

Walnut Mushroom Salad: Omit the sesame seeds and add ½ cup (125 mL) raw walnut halves and ½ cup (125 mL) Tahini Tzatziki (page 28). Toss until well coated.

Crunchy Asian Greens

This crunchy mix of fresh vegetables can be served on its own as a light lunch or with Lo Mein "Stir-Fry" (page 151) and Sesame Garlic Dressing (page 136) as an exotic main course.

**Makes
1 main-course or
2 side salads**

Tips

To remove the stem and string from a snap pea, pinch its bottom tip to get a grip on the stem. Twist the stem to loosen the string along the spine, pull the string up the straight side of the pea pod and then pinch it off and discard.

When following a completely raw food diet, look for sesame oil that is made from untoasted sesame seeds and is completely unrefined. It will be labeled "cold-pressed."

1 cup	finely sliced snow peas	250 mL
½ cup	snap peas, stems and strings removed (see Tips, left)	125 mL
3	baby bok choy, finely sliced	3
2 tbsp	cold-pressed sesame oil (untoasted; see Tips, left)	30 mL
2 tsp	freshly squeezed lemon juice	10 mL
¼ tsp	fine sea salt	1 mL

1. In a bowl, toss together snow peas, snap peas and bok choy. Add sesame oil, lemon juice and salt. Toss well. Set aside for 10 minutes, until softened. Serve immediately or transfer to an airtight container and refrigerate for up to 2 days.

Variation

Substitute 1 cup (250 mL) finely sliced napa cabbage for the baby bok choy and add 1 tsp (5 mL) raw white sesame seeds.

Red Pepper, Snap Pea and Ginger Cashew Salad

Fresh and tasty, this recipe will quickly become one of your go-to salads. Enjoy it as a side dish with Vegetable "Fried Rice" (page 165) or Kale Spring Rolls (page 158).

Makes 1 main-course or 2 side salads

Tips

To remove the skin from gingerroot with the least amount of waste, use the edge of a teaspoon. With a brushing motion, scrape off the skin to reveal the yellow root.

I prefer to use organic sea salt. This type of salt is classified as a whole food and is said to contain many trace minerals. If salt intake is something you are concerned about, feel free to use less than called for or omit it completely.

1 cup	finely sliced red bell pepper (about 2 medium)	250 mL
½ cup	snap peas, strings removed (about 10 to 15; see Tips, page 116)	125 mL
¾ cup	whole raw cashews	175 mL
3 tbsp	chopped gingerroot	45 mL
3 tbsp	cold-pressed sesame oil (untoasted; see Tips, page 116)	45 mL
¼ tsp	fine sea salt	1 mL

1. In a serving bowl, toss together red pepper, snap peas and cashews until well combined. Set aside.
2. In a food processor fitted with the metal blade, process ginger, sesame oil and salt until smooth.
3. Add ginger-sesame dressing to the vegetable mixture and toss until well coated. Serve immediately or cover and refrigerate for up to 2 days.

Variation

Green Pepper, Spinach and Ginger Cashew Salad: Substitute green bell pepper for the red pepper and 2 cups (500 mL) baby spinach for the snap peas. After tossing the vegetables with dressing in Step 3, set aside for 5 minutes to soften before serving.

Lemony Wilted Kale and Beets

This salad screams "fresh and healthy." Try it with Lemon Tahini Dressing (page 131) and some slices of fresh avocado.

....

**Makes
2 main-course or
4 side salads**

Tips

Black kale, also known as dinosaur kale or lacinato kale, is a nutritional powerhouse. If you cannot find black kale, use green kale (also known as curly kale).

Use a mandoline to slice the beets approximately ¼ inch (0.5 cm) thick. If you do not have a mandoline, substitute ½ cup (125 mL) shredded beets for the sliced beets.

1	bunch black kale, thinly sliced (see Tips, left)	1
1 cup	thinly sliced beets (see Tips, left)	250 mL
2 tbsp	freshly grated lemon zest	30 mL
3 tbsp	freshly squeezed lemon juice	45 mL
2 tbsp	cold-pressed (extra virgin) olive oil	30 mL
½ tsp	fine sea salt	2 mL

1. In a bowl, toss together kale, beets and lemon zest. Add lemon juice, olive oil and salt. Toss well. Set aside for 10 minutes, until softened. Serve immediately or transfer to an airtight container and refrigerate for up to 2 days.

Spicy Pear and Cabbage Salad

This simple yet satisfying salad is perfect on its own or served over a bed of fresh baby arugula.

**Makes
1 main-course or
2 side salads**

Tips

If your cabbage leaves have a tough spine running through the middle, use a paring knife to remove the more fibrous part.

Slicing the cabbage and pear to the same thickness will ensure that the salad is uniform in texture and taste. Using a mandoline will make this task easier.

If you prefer more heat, add up to ½ tsp (2 mL) cayenne pepper.

2 cups	finely sliced cabbage leaves (see Tips, left)	500 mL
1 cup	finely sliced pear (see Tips, left)	250 mL
2 tbsp	cold-pressed (extra virgin) olive oil	30 mL
2 tbsp	freshly squeezed lemon juice (see Tips, page 124)	30 mL
½ tsp	fine sea salt	2 mL
¼ tsp	cayenne pepper (see Tips, left)	1 mL

1. In a bowl, toss cabbage, pear, olive oil, lemon juice, salt and cayenne until well combined. Cover and set aside for 10 minutes, until softened. Serve immediately or cover and refrigerate for up to 2 days.

Variation

Substitute an equal quantity of finely sliced kale for the cabbage.

Asian Kale Slaw

This salad highlights the versatility of kale. Not only is it easy to prepare, it is also highly nutritious and filling.

Makes 2 main-course or 4 side salads

Tips

Kale comes in many different forms. The most common, green kale, is widely available. Black kale, which is also called dinosaur kale or lacinato kale, is reputed to be the most nutrient-dense.

Kale and collard leaves have a long, thick vein that runs through the center. When working with these vegetables, keep the soft vein at the top of the leaf intact. However, as you move toward the bottom (stem) end of the leaf, the vein becomes larger and tougher and needs to be removed. Lay the leaf flat on a cutting board and use a paring knife to remove the thick part of the vein; discard the vein portion. For this recipe, slice the remaining leafy green part into thin strips.

¼ cup	cold-pressed sesame oil (untoasted; see Tips, page 116)	60 mL
3 tbsp	filtered water	45 mL
3 tbsp	wheat-free tamari	45 mL
1 tbsp	raw agave nectar	15 mL
1	bunch black kale, stems removed, thinly sliced (see Tips, left)	1
1 tsp	raw sesame seeds	5 mL

1. In a blender, combine sesame oil, water, tamari and agave nectar. Blend at high speed until smooth.
2. In a bowl, toss kale with sesame seeds and dressing until well coated. Set aside for 5 minutes, until softened. Serve immediately or cover and refrigerate for up to 2 days.

Variation

Substitute ½ bunch of green (curly) kale for the black kale.

Shred-Me-Up Slaw

I love the simplicity of combining common ingredients to create a hearty, healthy dish that can be enjoyed as a snack or as a main course.

**Makes
1 main-course or
2 side salads**

Tip

I prefer to use organic sea salt. This type of salt is classified as a whole food and is said to contain many trace minerals. If salt intake is something you are concerned about, feel free to use less than called for or omit it completely.

½ cup	shredded carrot	125 mL
½ cup	shredded beet	125 mL
½ cup	finely sliced kale (see Tips, page 120)	125 mL
¼ cup	shredded squash	60 mL
3 tbsp	freshly squeezed lemon juice	45 mL
½ tsp	fine sea salt (see Tip, left)	2 mL

1. In a bowl, toss together carrot, beet, kale and squash. Add lemon juice and salt. Toss well. Set aside for 10 minutes, until softened. Serve immediately or transfer to an airtight container and refrigerate for up to 2 days.

Variations

Substitute an equal quantity of lime juice for the lemon juice and/or an equal quantity of finely sliced chard for the kale.

For a boost of protein, add 3 tbsp (45 mL) raw shelled hemp seeds.

Crunchy Cabbage and Carrot Slaw

This crunchy slaw will remind you of family picnics and summer barbecues. Enjoy, knowing that it contains none of the hidden ingredients in most store-bought coleslaws.

**Makes
1 main-course or
2 side salads**

Tips

For shredding small amounts of vegetables, use the side of a box grater. For larger amounts you can use the shredding attachment on your food processor.

When purchasing agave nectar, be sure to look for products labeled "raw." Most of the agave nectar on the market has been heated to a high temperature and so does not qualify as raw food. If you have concerns, ask your purveyor.

2 cups	shredded cabbage (see Tips, left)	500 mL
1 cup	shredded carrots	250 mL
¼ cup	freshly squeezed lemon juice	60 mL
3 tbsp	cold-pressed (extra virgin) olive oil	45 mL
2 tbsp	raw agave nectar (see Tips, left)	30 mL
¼ tsp	fine sea salt	1 mL

1. In a bowl, combine cabbage, carrots, lemon juice, olive oil, agave nectar and salt. Toss until well combined. Cover and set aside for 10 minutes, until softened. Serve immediately or cover and refrigerate for up to 3 days.

Variation

For a boost of protein, add ¼ cup (60 mL) whole raw cashews.

Mexican Jicama Slaw

Jicama is a refreshing vegetable that tastes like a blend of apple, celery and potato. In this salad it is mixed with cumin and chili powder for an authentic Mexican experience.

**Makes
1 main-course or
2 side salads**

Tips

Although extra virgin olive oil should, by definition, be cold-pressed, it is worth checking the label. Some olive oils are extracted using a centrifuge system, which spins the olives at a very high rate. This heats them and the resulting oil, depriving it of its raw status.

To peel the jicama, use a sharp chef's knife to cut a small slice from each end, exposing the flesh. Starting from the top, in a downward motion, cut away the dark brown skin around the flesh and discard.

Use a mandoline to slice the jicama approximately $\frac{1}{4}$ inch (0.5 cm) thick. Then stack the slices on a cutting board and, using a sharp chef's knife, cut into thin, even strips.

$\frac{1}{4}$ cup	cold-pressed (extra virgin) olive oil (see Tips, left)	60 mL
3 tbsp	freshly squeezed lime juice	45 mL
1 tsp	chili powder	5 mL
$\frac{1}{2}$ tsp	ground cumin	2 mL
$\frac{1}{4}$ tsp	fine sea salt	1 mL
2 cups	finely sliced peeled jicama (see Tips, left)	500 mL

1. In a food processor fitted with the metal blade, process olive oil, lime juice, chili powder, cumin and salt. Transfer to a bowl.
2. Add jicama to dressing and toss until well coated. Cover and set aside for 10 minutes, until softened. Serve immediately or cover and refrigerate for up to 2 days.

Sweet Pepper Slaw

This simple slaw is great served on its own or tossed with some Mexican Fiesta Dressing (page 27) for an exotic-tasting meal.

Makes
1 main-course or
2 side salads

Tips

To slice the peppers, use a sharp chef's knife to cut a small slice from each end. Stand the pepper upright and make a cut down one side from top to bottom. Lay the pepper on its side and gently pull it apart. Slide the knife tip flat against the flesh of the pepper to remove the membrane and seeds; discard the membrane and seeds. Lay the pepper flat and slice thinly.

To yield the maximum juice from citrus fruits, allow them to sit at room temperature for 30 minutes before juicing. Once the fruit is at room temperature, use the palm of your hand to roll it on the counter to release the juices before slicing and squeezing.

1 cup	finely sliced red bell pepper (see Tips, left)	250 mL
1 cup	finely sliced yellow bell pepper	250 mL
½ cup	fresh cilantro leaves, stems removed	125 mL
2 tbsp	cold-pressed (extra virgin) olive oil	30 mL
1 tbsp	freshly squeezed lemon juice (see Tips, left)	15 mL
¼ tsp	fine sea salt	1 mL

1. In a bowl, combine red and yellow peppers and cilantro. Add olive oil, lemon juice and salt and toss until well coated. Cover and set aside for 5 minutes, until softened. Serve immediately or cover and refrigerate for up to 2 days.

Variation

Substitute an equal quantity of fresh lime juice for the lemon juice.

Dressings

A typical salad dressing is made from refined oil, vinegar, refined salt and refined sugar. If you are using a store-bought version, it is also likely to contain preservatives. Thus, for many people, salad dressings are a guilty pleasure — but they don't need to be. You can immediately improve the nutritional profile of any dressing simply by using a heart-healthy cold-pressed organic oil. Healthy oils range from extra virgin olive oil to cold-pressed nut and seed oils such as walnut, hemp and flax. If you are worried that you are consuming too much oil, feel free to use less than the amount called for in the recipes, replace it with water or omit it completely. Be aware, however, that if you don't consume an adequate amount of fat you can end up with vitamin deficiencies. Your body requires a certain amount of fat to enable it to absorb the fat-soluble vitamins A, D, K and E. When reducing the quantity of fat, keep in mind that some recipes do require fat to work while others do not — experiment to find the balance that works for you. If you like a hint of sweetness, ingredients such as dates or raw agave nectar will do the trick while also adding nutrients. Use unrefined fine sea salt or seaweed to add a salty flavor. There's no reason why you can't enjoy your favorite dressing guilt-free.

You will find that the dressings in this chapter are very versatile. They can play the sidekick, as when Spicy Lime Avocado Dressing (page 132) dresses a main-course dish such as Squash Burrito (page 159). Or they can be the main attraction, for example, when a simple salad such as Lemony Wilted Kale and Beets (page 118) is enhanced by Creamy Herb Dressing (page 128) or Easy Italian Dressing (page 127).

I like to use a high-powered blender to make dressings because it allows me to add ingredients such as spinach or kale. If you have transitioned to a raw food diet, a high-powered blender is one of the most useful pieces of equipment to have (see page 15). Use a blender to add tasty and nutritious ingredients such as avocado, miso, fresh herbs, seeds or nuts.

Poured over a bed of greens or a more substantial mix of vegetables, the dressings in this chapter can dramatically improve the nutrient profile of any salad while helping to keep you feeling full and satisfied throughout the day.

Easy Italian Dressing

When I was a kid, I loved Italian salad dressing. I put it on everything from hot dogs and hamburgers to mac 'n' cheese. As an adult I have fallen in love with this healthier alternative made with unpasteurized apple cider vinegar, which may aid in digestion and provide healthy bacteria to improve the health status of your gut. Try this dressing over a big bowl of crisp romaine lettuce and juicy tomatoes.

**Makes
2 cups (500 mL)**

Tips

You may substitute 3 tbsp (45 mL) fresh oregano leaves for the dried.

I prefer to use organic sea salt. This type of salt is classified as a whole food and is said to contain many trace minerals. If salt intake is something you are concerned about, feel free to use less than called for or omit it completely.

¾ cup	cold-pressed (extra virgin) olive oil	175 mL
¼ cup	unpasteurized apple cider vinegar	60 mL
2 tbsp	filtered water	30 mL
1 tbsp	raw agave nectar	15 mL
1 tbsp	dried oregano (see Tips, left)	15 mL
1 tsp	fine sea salt	5 mL
2	cloves garlic	2

1. In a blender, combine olive oil, vinegar, water, agave nectar, oregano, salt and garlic. Blend at high speed until smooth. Serve immediately or cover and refrigerate for up to 7 days.

Variation

Substitute ⅓ cup (75 mL) freshly squeezed lemon juice for the vinegar.

Creamy Herb Dressing

Soft herbs such as basil and cilantro infuse bold flavor into dressings, dips and sauces. Serve this creamy dressing with some crisp fresh watercress or drizzle it over Caprese Stacked Salad (page 112).

	Makes 2 cups (500 mL)	

Tips

Although extra virgin olive oil should, by definition, be cold-pressed, it is worth checking the label. Some olive oils are extracted using a centrifuge system, which spins the olives at a very high rate. This heats the olives and the resulting oil, depriving it of its raw status.

To store fresh herbs, rinse well in cool water to remove any dirt, then dry in a salad spinner. Wrap in slightly damp paper towels and refrigerate for up to one week.

Typically a medium-sized lemon will yield about 3 tbsp (45 mL) fresh lemon juice.

1 cup	cold-pressed (extra virgin) olive oil (see Tips, left)	250 mL
½ cup	filtered water	125 mL
¼ cup	freshly squeezed lemon juice (see Tips, left)	60 mL
2 tsp	fine sea salt	10 mL
2	bunches fresh basil, roughly chopped	2
1	bunch fresh flat-leaf (Italian) parsley, stems removed, roughly chopped	1
1	bunch fresh cilantro, roughly chopped	1

1. In a blender, combine olive oil, water, lemon juice, salt, basil, parsley and cilantro. Blend at high speed until smooth. Serve immediately or cover and refrigerate for up to 4 days.

Variations

For a healthy boost of omega-3 fatty acids, substitute an equal amount of cold-pressed hemp oil for the olive oil, or use ½ cup (125 mL) olive oil and ½ cup (125 mL) cold-pressed flax oil.

Creamy Miso Dressing

This rich, creamy miso dressing gives salads an Asian flair. Pair it with finely sliced cabbage and baby bok choy or use it as a garnish for Lo Mein "Stir-Fry" (page 151).

**Makes
1¾ cups (425 mL)**

Tips

Although not a raw product, unpasteurized miso is often accepted in raw food diets because it is fermented, which provides healthy bacteria to aid in digestion. Brown rice miso is gluten-free and also contains vitamin B_{12}.

To remove the skin from a clove of garlic, use the butt end of a chef's knife to press firmly but gently on the clove to loosen the skin. Using your index finger and thumb, carefully ease off the skin.

1 cup	filtered water	250 mL
½ cup	cold-pressed (extra virgin) olive oil	125 mL
¼ cup	unpasteurized brown rice miso (see Tips, left)	60 mL
2 tbsp	raw agave nectar	30 mL
1 tbsp	wheat-free tamari	15 mL
2	cloves garlic (see Tips, left)	2

1. In a blender, combine water, olive oil, miso, agave nectar, tamari and garlic. Blend at high speed until smooth. Serve immediately or cover and refrigerate for up to 5 days.

Variation

For a healthy boost of omega-3 fatty acids, replace ¼ cup (60 mL) of the olive oil with ¼ cup (60 mL) cold-pressed flax oil.

Lemon Dill Cucumber Dressing

This light and refreshing dressing is a mixture of cooling cucumber, fresh and flavorful dill weed and tangy lemon. When the temperature climbs, I like to serve this with a big bowl of fresh baby spinach, juicy cherry tomatoes and creamy avocado.

**Makes
1¼ cups (300 mL)**

Tips

Using a food processor gives this dressing a slight texture, which I prefer. If you'd like a smoother dressing, by all means use a blender.

Although extra virgin olive oil should, by definition, be cold-pressed, it is worth checking the label. Some olive oils are extracted using a centrifuge system, which spins the olives at a very high rate. This heats the olives and the resulting oil, depriving it of its raw status.

1 cup	chopped cucumber	250 mL
½ cup	cold-pressed (extra virgin) olive oil (see Tips, left)	125 mL
¼ cup	freshly squeezed lemon juice	60 mL
¼ cup	filtered water	60 mL
1 tsp	fine sea salt	5 mL
1	bunch fresh dill, stems removed, roughly chopped	1
2	cloves garlic	2

1. In a food processor fitted with the metal blade, process cucumber, olive oil, lemon juice, water, salt, dill and garlic until smooth, stopping motor to scrape down sides of work bowl as necessary. Serve immediately or cover and refrigerate for up to 3 days.

Variation

Substitute 2 bunches of fresh basil for the dill weed.

Lemon Tahini Dressing

This creamy, lemony dressing is perfect for when you are craving something rich and delicious.

Makes
1 cup (250 mL)

Tips

Tahini is a paste or butter made from ground sesame seeds that is similar to peanut or almond butter. Most store-bought tahini is made from sesame seeds that have been roasted, depriving it of its raw status. If you are following a strictly raw diet, be sure to look for products labeled "raw."

As with most nut butters, the oil in tahini has a tendency to separate in the jar. Be sure to mix it well before using. If not, your dressing could be thinner than desired.

¾ cup	filtered water	175 mL
½ cup	raw tahini (see Tips, left)	125 mL
⅓ cup	freshly squeezed lemon juice	75 mL
1 tsp	fine sea salt	5 mL
3	cloves garlic	3

1. In a blender, combine water, tahini, lemon juice, salt and garlic. Blend at high speed until smooth. Serve immediately or cover and refrigerate for up to 5 days.

Variations

Herbed Lemon Tahini Dressing: Add ½ cup (125 mL) chopped fresh parsley leaves and ¼ cup (60 mL) chopped fresh basil leaves.

Smoky Tahini Dressing: Add 2 tsp (10 mL) sweet smoked paprika.

Spicy Lime Avocado Dressing

This dressing combines aromatic spices, rich avocado and tart lime. I like to toss it with crisp romaine lettuce and juicy wedges of tomato and cucumber.

¾ cup	filtered water	175 mL
¼ cup	freshly squeezed lime juice	60 mL
½	medium avocado (see Tips, left)	½
1 tbsp	raw agave nectar	15 mL
2 tsp	chili powder	10 mL
1 tsp	fine sea salt	5 mL
1	clove garlic	1

**Makes
1 cup (250 mL)**

Tips

The texture of this dressing will depend on the ripeness of the avocado. If it's not thick enough for your liking, add 1 tbsp (15 mL) chopped avocado and blend at high speed until smooth. Continue to add avocado until you reach the desired consistency.

To remove the pit from an avocado, use a paring knife to remove the nib at the top. Insert the blade of the knife where the nib was and turn the avocado from top to bottom to cut it in half lengthwise. Twist the two halves apart. Stick the knife into the pit and, with one motion, turn it 90 degrees, pulling out the pit as you twist the knife.

1. In a blender, combine water, lime juice, avocado, agave nectar, chili powder, salt and garlic. Blend at high speed until smooth. Serve immediately or cover and refrigerate for up to 3 days.

Variation

Summery Lemon Avocado Dressing: Substitute freshly squeezed lemon juice for the lime juice and ½ cup (125 mL) fresh basil leaves for the chili powder.

Tomato Basil Dressing

For me, few things say "summer" more than tomatoes and basil. This simple dressing delivers a pop of flavor that pairs well with crisp romaine lettuce and a drizzle of Creamy Alfredo Sauce (page 24).

(page 24)

Makes
Makes **1½ cups (375 mL)**

Tips

If you can, use heirloom tomatoes for this dressing. Heirloom tomatoes have a meatier texture and are more flavorful than most commercial tomatoes. Look for varieties such as Green Zebra, Oaxacan Jewel, Brandywine and Purple Russian. Check out your local farmers' market to see what is available.

While wheat-free tamari is not raw, it is gluten-free. The raw alternative for tamari, nama shoyu, does contain gluten. If you are following a completely raw diet and can tolerate gluten, by all means substitute an equal quantity of nama shoyu.

1 cup	chopped tomatoes (see Tips, left)	250 mL
½ cup	cold-pressed (extra virgin) olive oil	125 mL
¼ cup	filtered water	60 mL
3 tbsp	wheat-free tamari (see Tips, left)	45 mL
2	cloves garlic	2
2	bunches fresh basil, roughly chopped	2

1. In a blender, combine tomatoes, olive oil, water, tamari, garlic and basil. Blend at high speed until smooth. Serve immediately or cover and refrigerate for up to 4 days.

Smoked Paprika and Red Pepper Dressing

I love making this dressing in cooler weather, when I crave big salads topped with nuts, seeds and avocado. It's a perfect blend of smoky paprika and sweet red peppers that gets its slightly sweet-and-salty undertone from sea salt and agave nectar.

Makes 2½ cups (625 mL)

Tips

Red peppers are extremely nutritious. They contain high levels of carotene, an antioxidant, and vitamin C.

To slice the peppers before chopping, use a sharp chef's knife to cut a small slice from each end. Stand the pepper upright and make a cut down one side, from top to bottom. Lay the pepper on its side and gently pull it apart. Slide the knife tip flat against the flesh of the pepper to remove the membrane and seeds; discard the membrane and seeds. Lay the pepper flat and slice thinly.

¾ cup	filtered water	175 mL
2 cups	chopped red bell peppers (see Tips, left)	500 mL
¼ cup	cold-pressed (extra virgin) olive oil	60 mL
2 tbsp	raw agave nectar	30 mL
1 tbsp	smoked sweet paprika	15 mL
1 tsp	fine sea salt	5 mL

1. In a blender, combine water, red peppers, olive oil, agave nectar, paprika and salt. Blend at high speed until smooth. Serve immediately or cover and refrigerate for up to 3 days.

Variations

Substitute 2 tbsp (30 mL) wheat-free tamari for the salt.

Southwest Red Pepper Dressing: Substitute 2 tsp (10 mL) chili powder for the paprika and add 1 tsp (5 mL) ground cumin.

Curried Carrot Dressing

This dressing is a fragrant blend of aromatic curry powder, tart lime and sweet carrot. Enjoy it tossed with crisp lettuce mixed with raisins or dates and fresh, juicy apple slices.

Makes
1¾ cups (425 mL)

Tips

To ensure a smooth dressing, chop the carrot very finely before adding it to the blender.

Carrots are extremely high in beta-carotene, a carotenoid that your body converts to vitamin A. Because smoking and drinking alcohol reduce the levels of beta-carotene in the blood, taking in adequate amounts of this nutrient is recommended if you consume alcohol on a regular basis and/or smoke tobacco.

¾ cup	cold-pressed (extra virgin) olive oil	175 mL
¾ cup	filtered water	175 mL
½ cup	finely chopped peeled carrot (see Tips, left)	125 mL
¼ cup	freshly squeezed lime juice	60 mL
1 tbsp	curry powder	15 mL
½ tsp	fine sea salt	2 mL
1	clove garlic	1

1. In a blender, combine olive oil, water, carrot, lime juice, curry powder, salt and garlic. Blend at high speed until smooth. Serve immediately or cover and refrigerate for up to 3 days.

Variation

Curried Coconut Carrot and Ginger Dressing: Substitute an equal amount of melted coconut oil for the olive oil and add 2 tbsp (30 mL) chopped gingerroot.

Coconut Garlic Dressing

Rich coconut and aromatic garlic are the stars of this dressing. Enjoy this with dark green leafy vegetables such as kale or mustard greens.

Makes 1½ cups (375 mL)

Tips

Coconut oil is solid at room temperature but has a melting point of 76°F (24°C), so it is easy to liquefy. To melt it, place in a shallow glass bowl over a pot of simmering water.

If the garlic cloves you are using are large, reduce the amount indicated to 4 cloves. If they are small, increase to 8 cloves.

¾ cup	filtered water	175 mL
½ cup	melted coconut oil (see Tips, left)	125 mL
3 tbsp	wheat-free tamari	45 mL
2 tsp	raw agave nectar	10 mL
¼ cup	roughly chopped flat-leaf (Italian) parsley leaves	60 mL
6	cloves garlic (see Tips, left)	6

1. In a blender, combine water, coconut oil, tamari, agave nectar, parsley and garlic. Blend at high speed until smooth. Serve immediately or cover and store at room temperature for up to 3 days.

Sesame Garlic Dressing

In this dressing, raw tahini and sesame oil create a rich sesame flavor that, mixed with garlic, pairs well with light leafy greens such as spinach or arugula.

Makes 1½ cups (375 mL)

Tip

To remove the skin from a clove of garlic, use the butt end of a chef's knife to press firmly but gently on the clove to loosen the skin. Using your index finger and thumb, carefully ease off the skin.

½ cup	filtered water	125 mL
¼ cup	raw tahini (see Tips, page 131)	60 mL
¼ cup	sesame oil (untoasted)	60 mL
3 tbsp	freshly squeezed lemon juice	45 mL
2 tbsp	raw sesame seeds	30 mL
1 tsp	fine sea salt	5 mL
3 to 4	cloves garlic (see Tip, left)	3 to 4

1. In a blender, combine water, tahini, sesame oil, lemon juice, sesame seeds, salt and garlic. Blend at high speed until smooth. Serve immediately or cover and refrigerate for up to 4 days.

Orange Chile Dressing

One of my favorite flavor combinations is spicy and sweet. This blend of dried chile and juicy orange pairs well with bitter vegetables such as radicchio, endive or dandelion leaves.

**Makes
2 cups (500 mL)**

Tips

To prepare the orange for this recipe, place the fruit on a cutting board and remove a bit of skin from the top and bottom to create a flat surface — this will reveal the thickness of the pith. Using a sharp knife in a downward motion, remove the skin and the pith. Shave off any remaining bits of pith, then cut between the membranes to produce wedges of pure citrus flesh.

Apple cider vinegar has long been used in folk medicine. It is a great digestive aid, among its other benefits. When purchasing apple cider vinegar, make sure that it is raw, was made from organically grown apples and contains the "mother," which is a source of healthy bacteria and enzymes.

1 cup	orange segments (see Tips, left)	250 mL
1/2 cup	cold-pressed (extra virgin) olive oil	125 mL
1/4 cup	unpasteurized apple cider vinegar (see Tips, left)	60 mL
3 tbsp	filtered water	45 mL
3 tbsp	raw agave nectar	45 mL
2 tbsp	hot pepper flakes	30 mL
1 tsp	fine sea salt	5 mL

1. In a blender, combine orange segments, olive oil, vinegar, water, agave nectar, hot pepper flakes and salt. Blend at high speed until smooth. Serve immediately or cover and refrigerate for up to 3 days.

Variation

For a spicier dressing, add 1/4 cup (60 mL) chopped seeded jalapeño pepper.

Mango Ginger Cilantro Dressing

During the summer I love to serve big fresh green salads with this light, sweet dressing. The mango gives it a wonderful creamy texture, perfect with crisp veggies such as cucumber, cabbage or sweet peppers.

....

Makes 1⅓ cups (325 mL)

Tips

To peel and chop a mango, cut a small slice from the top and bottom of the fruit to make flat ends. Using a vegetable peeler, carefully peel away the skin. Stand the mango on a cutting board and, using a chef's knife, run the blade through the flesh, taking approximately three slices from each of the four sides. When you get close to the stone, use a paring knife to remove any remaining flesh from around it.

Cilantro, like all herbs, contains an abundance of phytonutrients with antioxidant properties. Early research suggests that it may help with digestion, ease bloating and relieve gas. To store fresh cilantro, rinse well in cool water to remove any dirt and dry in a salad spinner. Wrap in slightly damp paper towels and refrigerate for up to one week.

⅔ cup	cold-pressed (extra virgin) olive oil	150 mL
½ cup	chopped mango (see Tips, left)	125 mL
½ cup	roughly chopped fresh cilantro leaves	125 mL
¼ cup	filtered water	60 mL
¼ cup	chopped peeled gingerroot	60 mL
1 tsp	fine sea salt	5 mL

1. In a blender, combine olive oil, mango, cilantro, water, ginger and salt. Blend at high speed until smooth. Serve immediately or cover and refrigerate for up to 3 days.

Ginger Apricot Dressing

This dressing's blend of sweet, rich apricots and spicy ginger pairs well with fresh cilantro, apples, squash or sweet potato. Try it with a Squash Burrito (page 159) or Sweet Potato Enchilada (page 160).

1 cup	filtered water	250 mL
1/3 cup	cold-pressed (extra virgin) olive oil	75 mL
1/4 cup	dried apricots, soaked (see Tips, left)	60 mL
1/4 cup	chopped peeled gingerroot	60 mL
3 tbsp	wheat-free tamari	45 mL
2 tbsp	raw agave nectar	30 mL

Makes
1½ cups (375 mL)

Tips

To soak the apricots, place in a bowl and cover with 2 cups (500 mL) hot water. Set aside for 10 minutes, until softened. Drain, discarding soaking liquid.

When purchasing dried apricots, make sure to look for ones that are darker in color. This means that they have not been treated with sulfites to preserve color. Read the label to be sure they are sulfite-free, or ask your purveyor if you have concerns.

1. In a blender, combine water, olive oil, apricots, ginger, tamari and agave nectar. Blend at high speed until smooth. Serve immediately or cover and refrigerate for up to 3 days.

Berry Vinaigrette

Few things say "summer" more than fresh berries. Use this to dress up a big bowl of baby spinach topped with fresh blueberries, almonds, shredded coconut and avocado.

**Makes
1¾ cups (425 mL)**

Tips

Although extra virgin olive oil should, by definition, be cold-pressed, it is worth checking the label. Some olive oils are extracted using a centrifuge system, which spins the olives at a very high rate. This heats the olives and the resulting oil, depriving it of its raw status.

Typically a medium-sized lemon will yield about 3 tbsp (45 mL) fresh lemon juice.

¾ cup	cold-pressed (extra virgin) olive oil (see Tips, left)	175 mL
½ cup	filtered water	125 mL
¼ cup	freshly squeezed lemon juice (see Tips, left)	60 mL
1 cup	blueberries	250 mL
½ cup	raspberries	125 mL
¼ tsp	fine sea salt	1 mL

1. In a blender, combine olive oil, water, lemon juice, blueberries, raspberries and salt. Blend at high speed until smooth. Serve immediately or cover and refrigerate for up to 2 days.

Variation

Substitute an equal amount of chopped hulled strawberries for the blueberries.

Pasta and Noodles

When most people think of pasta, they visualize soft wheat-based noodles swimming in a pool of bubbling sauce. While raw pasta recipes may not be served steaming hot, it is possible to create dishes that are entirely satisfying. In fact, raw "pasta" is one of the most common dishes in raw cuisine. From fettuccini and ravioli to gnocchi and spaghetti, nearly any type of traditional pasta dish can be re-created using fresh vegetables and a few special techniques.

You can slice vegetables thinly on a mandoline or by using a Y-shaped (slingshot) vegetable peeler. I like to use a spiral vegetable slicer — often referred to as a spiralizer — to quickly cut vegetables into spaghettini. Marinating thinly sliced vegetables then helps to soften them.

The natural shape of cylindrical ingredients such as carrots, parsnips and daikon radish is perfect for creating fettuccini, linguine or angel hair pasta, as you'll see in my recipe for Angel Hair Beets and Greens (page 146). Sliced beets, jicama and rutabaga make fantastic wrappers for ravioli, manicotti or pot stickers — try Jicama Pot Stickers (page 152). Zucchini is wonderfully versatile; it can be used to make spaghetti or sheets for lasagna. Spaghetti and Seed Balls (page 143) is my take on a classic Italian dish. All of these are fantastic served with sauces you can find in the "In the Pantry" chapter (page 17). Try Cashew Almond Gnocchi (page 149) tossed with a big helping of Chunky Tomato Marinara Sauce (page 25), or Celery Root Ravioli (page 147) with Green Pesto (page 26).

Raw pasta can create an entirely gratifying meal when prepared correctly. With just a little imagination and some fresh vegetables, your mealtime possibilities are limitless.

Spaghetti and Seed Balls

This take on the Italian classic uses fresh zucchini noodles, rich tomato marinara sauce and "meatballs" made from sunflower seeds, creamy nut butter and Italian seasoning.

Makes 2 servings

Tips

You may substitute 1 tsp (5 mL) dried oregano and $\frac{1}{2}$ tsp (2 mL) dried basil for the Italian seasoning.

When purchasing dried herbs, try to buy organic versions. Always store dried herbs in an airtight container in a cool, dry place away from light.

A spiral vegetable slicer (spiralizer) is one of the most common tools used in raw food preparation. You can find them in most well-stocked natural foods stores or through specialty suppliers. The smallest blade will make spaghetti-sized noodles, the medium blade will make half-moon noodles and the largest blade will make thick, dense noodles.

- Spiral vegetable slicer, fitted with the smallest blade (see Tips, left)

2	large zucchini	2
1 cup	raw sunflower seeds	250 mL
2 tsp	Italian seasoning (see Tips, left)	10 mL
$\frac{1}{2}$ tsp	fine sea salt	2 mL
$\frac{1}{4}$ cup	raw almond butter	60 mL
1 cup	Chunky Tomato Marinara Sauce (page 25, or Variation, page 148), divided	250 mL

1. Using a sharp chef's knife, remove a small portion from each end of the zucchini to create a flat surface. Using spiralizer fitted with the smallest blade, secure zucchini on prongs. Rotate crank while gently pushing zucchini toward blade to create long strands of "pasta." Transfer noodles to a bowl.

2. In a food processor fitted with the metal blade, process sunflower seeds, Italian seasoning and salt until roughly combined (you want to retain some texture). Transfer to a bowl. Add almond butter and mix until well combined.

3. Using a tablespoon (15 mL), scoop up 8 equal portions of the mixture. Using the palms of your hands, roll each into a ball and set aside.

4. Divide zucchini noodles into 2 portions and arrange each on a serving plate. Top each with $\frac{1}{2}$ cup (125 mL) marinara sauce and 4 seed balls. Serve immediately.

Variations

For added flavor I like to add 2 tbsp (30 mL) nutritional yeast along with the sunflower seeds, Italian seasoning and salt in Step 2.

Substitute an equal amount of raw pumpkin seeds for the sunflower seeds.

Zucchini Spaghetti with Lemon and Herbs

I love the versatility of zucchini noodles in raw food cuisine. In this dish they are tossed with rich olive oil, aromatic fresh herbs and zesty lemon.

Makes 2 servings

Tips

A spiral vegetable slicer (spiralizer) is one of the most common tools used in raw food preparation. You can find them in most well-stocked natural foods stores or through specialty suppliers. The smallest blade will make spaghetti-sized noodles, the medium blade will make half-moon noodles and the largest blade will make thick, dense noodles.

I prefer to use organic sea salt. This type of salt is classified as a whole food and is said to contain many trace minerals. If salt intake is something you are concerned about, feel free to use less than called for or omit it completely.

- **Spiral vegetable slicer, fitted with the smallest blade (see Tips, left)**

2	large zucchini	2
2	bunches flat-leaf (Italian) parsley, stems removed, roughly chopped	2
¼ cup	cold-pressed (extra virgin) olive oil	60 mL
1 tbsp	lemon zest	15 mL
¼ cup	freshly squeezed lemon juice	60 mL
½ tsp	fine sea salt (see Tips, left)	2 mL

1. Using a sharp chef's knife, remove a small portion from each end of the zucchini to create a flat surface. Using spiralizer fitted with the smallest blade, secure zucchini on prongs. Rotate crank while gently pushing zucchini toward blade to create long strands of "pasta." Transfer noodles to a bowl.

2. In a food processor fitted with the metal blade, combine parsley, olive oil, lemon zest and juice and salt. Process until smooth, stopping motor to scrape down sides of work bowl as necessary. Add to zucchini noodles and toss until well coated. Serve immediately.

Variations

Try spiralizing other vegetables or fruits — such as carrots, parsnips, beets, apples or squash — in place of the zucchini in this recipe.

Substitute 3 bunches of fresh cilantro, roughly chopped, for the parsley and add other vegetables, such as broccoli florets, cauliflower florets or shredded carrot.

For a boost of protein, add ¼ cup (60 mL) raw shelled hemp seeds.

Zucchini Noodles in Chunky Tomato Marinara Sauce: Substitute 2 cups (500 mL) Chunky Tomato Marinara Sauce (page 25) for the parsley, olive oil, lemon zest and juice, and salt in Step 2.

Zucchini Fettuccini Alfredo

This Alfredo is as delicious as its traditional counterpart. Rich, creamy cashews stand in for the heavy cream, and nutritional yeast provides a cheesy flavor without any saturated fat.

Makes 1 serving

Tips

Nutritional yeast flakes can be found in well-stocked supermarkets and natural foods stores. Although not a raw product, nutritional yeast is fortified with vitamin B_{12} and helps to produce umami, a savory flavor sometimes lacking in vegetarian cuisine.

A Y-shaped (slingshot) vegetable peeler glides easily down zucchini to make these noodles, but by all means use a regular vegetable peeler if that is what you have.

1/2 cup	whole raw almonds	125 mL
2 tbsp	nutritional yeast (see Tips, left)	30 mL
1/4 tsp	fine sea salt	1 mL
1	large zucchini, ends trimmed	1
1/2 cup	Creamy Alfredo Sauce (page 24 or Variations, below)	125 mL
Pinch	ground nutmeg	Pinch

1. In a food processor fitted with the metal blade, process almonds, nutritional yeast and salt until flourlike in consistency (be careful not to overprocess — you do not want to make a paste). Transfer to a bowl and set aside.

2. Using a vegetable peeler, peel zucchini lengthwise into long, thin strips, down each of the four sides (see Tips, left). Stack strips (peels and flesh) on top of each other and, using a sharp chef's knife, cut lengthwise into strips approximately 1/2 inch (1 cm) wide. Transfer to a bowl.

3. Combine zucchini strips with Alfredo sauce and three-quarters of the almond mixture. Mix until well combined. Transfer to a serving plate and garnish with remaining almond mixture and a pinch of ground nutmeg.

Variations

If you don't have Creamy Alfredo Sauce on hand, here's a substitute that produces a smaller quantity: In a blender, combine 1/2 cup (125 mL) raw cashews, 1/2 cup (125 mL) filtered water, 2 tbsp (30 mL) nutritional yeast, 1 tbsp (15 mL) freshly squeezed lemon juice, 1/2 tsp (2 mL) fine sea salt and 1/4 to 1/2 clove garlic. Blend at high speed until smooth.

To make this dish even more rich and filling, substitute raw walnut halves for the almonds in Step 1.

Angel Hair Beets and Greens

This is a simple way to enjoy a delicious raw pasta dish, using fresh beets.

Tips

I prefer to use organic sea salt. This type of salt is classified as a whole food and is said to contain many trace minerals. If salt intake is something you are concerned about, feel free to use less than called for or omit it completely.

Typically beets can be purchased with or without the greens attached. If you are unable to find beets with the greens attached, substitute 2 cups (500 mL) finely sliced kale for the beet greens.

Use any type of beet for this recipe. Red, golden and candy cane beets work equally well.

- **Mandoline**

¼ cup	cold-pressed (extra virgin) olive oil, divided	60 mL
¼ cup	freshly squeezed lemon juice, divided	60 mL
1 tsp	fine sea salt, divided	5 mL
¼ cup	raw shelled hemp seeds	60 mL
3 tbsp	filtered water	45 mL
3 tbsp	nutritional yeast	45 mL
2	medium beets, greens attached (see Tips, left)	2

1. In a blender, combine 2 tbsp (30 mL) olive oil, 2 tbsp (30 mL) lemon juice, ½ tsp (2 mL) salt, hemp seeds, water and nutritional yeast. Blend at high speed until smooth. Cover and set aside.

2. Remove greens from beets, cutting off and discarding stems. Set leaves aside. Using a vegetable peeler, peel beets. Using mandoline, slice beets approximately ⅛ inch (3 mm) thick. Stack slices on top of each other and, using a sharp chef's knife, cut into strips approximately ⅛ inch (3 mm) wide. Place in a bowl, cover and set aside.

3. On cutting board, roll up beet greens to form cylindrical shapes. Using a sharp chef's knife, cut cylinders into strips approximately ⅛ inch (3 mm) thick.

4. In a bowl, combine greens, beets and remaining olive oil, lemon juice and salt. Toss until well combined. Cover and set aside for 5 minutes, until softened.

5. Toss hemp seed sauce with beet mixture. Serve immediately or cover and refrigerate for up to 2 days.

Variations

Replace the hemp seed sauce with 2 cups (500 mL) Creamy Alfredo Sauce (page 24), Chunky Tomato Marinara Sauce (page 25) or Tahini Tzatziki (page 28).

Celery Root Ravioli

Here's a simple way to create delicious ravioli using only a few ingredients. Celery root gives this dish a deep, rich flavor.

Makes 4 servings

Tips

You may replace the olive oil with any organic cold-pressed oil such as flax, hemp, chia, pumpkin or avocado oil.

To soak the cashews, place in a bowl and cover with 2 cups (500 mL) water. Cover and set aside for 10 minutes. Drain, discarding soaking water, and rinse under cold running water until the water runs clear.

- **Mandoline**

1	medium celery root, peeled	1
¼ cup	cold-pressed (extra virgin) olive oil (see Tips, left)	60 mL
¼ cup	freshly squeezed lemon juice, divided	60 mL
¾ tsp	fine sea salt, divided	3 mL
1 cup	whole raw cashews, soaked (see Tips, left)	250 mL
¼ cup	filtered water	60 mL
2 tbsp	nutritional yeast	30 mL

1. Using mandoline, slice celery root crosswise approximately $\frac{1}{16}$ inch (2 mm) thick. Transfer slices to a bowl.

2. Add olive oil, 2 tbsp (30 mL) lemon juice and ¼ tsp (1 mL) salt to celery root slices. Toss until well combined. Cover and set aside for 10 minutes, until softened.

3. In a food processor fitted with the metal blade, combine soaked cashews, water, nutritional yeast and remaining lemon juice and salt. Process until nuts are roughly chopped (you want to retain some texture). Set aside.

4. Place half of the celery root slices on a flat work surface. Spoon 1 to 2 tbsp (15 to 30 mL) cashew filling in center of each. Top with another slice of celery root. Using your hands, gently push down edges around filling to squeeze out any excess air and form a ravioli shape. Serve immediately or cover and refrigerate for up to 4 days.

Variations

Substitute an equal quantity of beets, turnip or rutabaga for the celery root.

Eggplant Manicotti

This is a delicious — and healthy — take on an Italian classic. The eggplant's rich texture soaks up the chunky tomato sauce, and slicing it paper-thin makes it easier to soften and roll around the creamy cashew cheese.

Makes 2 servings

Tips

Use a mandoline to slice the eggplant lengthwise into pieces approximately $\frac{1}{16}$ inch (2 mm) thick.

Salting the eggplant removes any bitterness and helps to soften it, a process that is completed by the marinating.

You can substitute zucchini for the eggplant: Cut zucchini into slices $\frac{1}{8}$ inch (3 mm) thick. Sprinkle with a pinch of fine sea salt and $\frac{1}{2}$ tsp (2 mL) chopped fresh thyme leaves, then drizzle with 1 to 2 tsp (5 to 10 mL) cold-pressed (extra virgin) olive oil. Set aside for 10 to 12 minutes, until softened. Continue with Step 4.

- **8-inch (20 cm) square glass baking dish**

1	medium eggplant, peeled and thinly sliced (see Tips, left)	1
$\frac{1}{4}$ cup	filtered water	60 mL
$\frac{1}{4}$ cup	freshly squeezed lemon juice	60 mL
3 tbsp	cold-pressed (extra virgin) olive oil	45 mL
2 tsp	fine sea salt, divided	10 mL
1 cup	Herbed Cashew Cheese (page 20)	250 mL
$\frac{1}{2}$ cup	Chunky Tomato Marinara Sauce (page 25 or Variation, below)	125 mL

1. Lay eggplant strips on a flat surface and generously sprinkle with $\frac{1}{2}$ tsp (2 mL) sea salt. Turn over and repeat. Set aside for 3 to 4 minutes. Gently rinse each eggplant strip under running water and pat dry.

2. In a blender, combine water, lemon juice, olive oil and 1 tsp (5 mL) salt. Blend at high speed until smooth.

3. In baking dish, arrange eggplant slices in a single layer. Pour lemon-and-oil mixture overtop, making sure eggplant is well coated. Cover and set aside for 8 to 10 minutes, until softened.

4. Remove eggplant from soaking liquid and pat dry. Place eggplant slices on a flat surface. Spread bottom third of each slice with 1 to 2 tbsp (15 to 30 mL) cashew cheese. Starting at bottom of each slice, roll up in jelly-roll fashion around cheese. Place rolls, seam side down, in baking dish. Top with marinara sauce. Serve immediately or cover and refrigerate for up to 2 days.

Variation

If you don't have Chunky Tomato Marinara Sauce on hand, here's a substitute that makes a smaller quantity: In a blender, combine 1 cup (250 mL) chopped tomato, $\frac{1}{4}$ cup (60 mL) sundried tomatoes, 2 tbsp (30 mL) cold-pressed extra virgin olive oil, 1 tbsp (15 mL) freshly squeezed lemon juice, 1 tsp (5 mL) dried basil leaves, $\frac{1}{8}$ tsp (0.5 mL) fine sea salt and 1 clove garlic. Blend until smooth.

Cashew Almond Gnocchi

I love serving these gnocchi with Green Pesto (page 26) and a side of Chunky Cucumber Corn Salad (page 113). The rich texture of the gnocchi is best paired with light sauces that have a zesty tang.

Makes about 40 gnocchi

Tips

When purchasing nuts, be sure to look for products labeled "raw." Most of the nuts on the market have been roasted and do not qualify as raw food. If you have concerns, ask your purveyor.

To grind flax seeds, place ¼ cup (60 mL) whole flax seeds in a blender or spice grinder and process until they become flourlike in consistency. Cover and refrigerate any extra ground flax seeds for up to 1 month.

If your dough is too sticky, add ground golden flax seeds, 1 tsp (5 mL) at a time, to help absorb excess moisture.

¾ cup	whole raw almonds	175 mL
1 cup	whole raw cashews	250 mL
1 tbsp	nutritional yeast	15 mL
½ tsp	fine sea salt	2 mL
¼ cup	filtered water	60 mL
1 tbsp	ground flax seeds (see Tips, left)	15 mL

1. In a food processor fitted with the metal blade, process almonds until flourlike in consistency (be careful not to overprocess — you do not want to make a paste). Transfer to a bowl.

2. In same work bowl, process cashews, nutritional yeast and salt until roughly chopped, so that mixture resembles chunky flour. With the motor running, drizzle in water and continue to process for 30 seconds or until a paste forms. Add to almonds.

3. Add flax seeds and mix well to form a slightly sticky dough (see Tips, left). Divide dough into 4 equal portions.

4. Using the palms of your hands, roll each portion of dough into a cylinder approximately 1 inch (2.5 cm) in diameter and 8 inches (20 cm) long. Cut each cylinder into approximately 10 equal pieces. Toss with 1 cup (250 mL) of your favorite sauce and serve, or transfer to an airtight container and refrigerate for up to 5 days.

Variations

Try adding other seasonings in Step 3, such as 2 tsp (10 mL) freshly grated lemon zest or 1 tsp (5 mL) dried basil.

This dish is also delicious with Chunky Tomato Marinara Sauce (page 25 or Variation, page 148).

Carrot Pad Thai

This take on the classic dish uses carrots to stand in for the rice noodles and an aromatic sauce made with almond butter as a base for delivering the fresh, bold flavors of Thai food.

Tips

A Y-shaped (slingshot) vegetable peeler glides easily down carrots to make these noodles, but by all means use a regular vegetable peeler if that is what you have.

I prefer to use organic sea salt. This type of salt is classified as a whole food and is said to contain many trace minerals. If salt intake is something you are concerned about, feel free to use less than called for or omit it completely.

4	large carrots	4
1/4 tsp	fine sea salt	1 mL
1/2 cup	finely sliced red bell pepper	125 mL
1/4 cup	broccoli florets	60 mL
1/4 cup	bean sprouts	60 mL
1/2 cup	Quick Thai Cream Sauce (page 23 or Variations, below)	125 mL

1. Using a vegetable peeler, peel carrots into long, thin strips (see Tips, left). Stack strips on top of each other and, using a sharp chef's knife, cut lengthwise into strips approximately 1/8 inch (3 mm) wide. Place strips in a bowl, add salt and toss until well combined.

2. Add red pepper, broccoli, bean sprouts and cream sauce. Toss until well combined. Serve immediately or cover and refrigerate for up to 2 days.

Variations

If you do not have Quick Thai Cream Sauce on hand, substitute a mixture of 3 tbsp (45 mL) fresh lime juice, 2 tbsp (30 mL) raw agave nectar, 1 tbsp (15 mL) wheat-free tamari and a pinch of cayenne pepper.

Substitute an equal quantity of daikon radish for the carrots.

Lo Mein "Stir-Fry"

This easy take on a stir-fry is a fast and delicious way to get more raw veggies into your diet. The slightly sweet and gingery sauce mimics the flavors of Asian takeaway noodles.

Tip

To clean mushrooms, use a damp cloth to brush any dirt from the surface. Never clean mushrooms with water. They are like sponges — they will absorb the water and turn gray.

- Mandoline

1	large carrot, peeled, top and bottom removed	1
½ cup	bean sprouts	125 mL
½ cup	thinly sliced snow peas	125 mL
½ cup	thinly sliced mushrooms (see Tip, left)	125 mL
½ cup	thinly sliced cabbage	125 mL
½ cup	Teriyaki Sauce (page 22 or Variations, below)	125 mL

1. Using mandoline, slice carrot into long, thin strips approximately ⅛ inch (3 mm) thick. Lay the strips on top of each other and, using a sharp chef's knife, cut lengthwise into strips approximately ⅛ inch (3 mm) wide to create carrot noodles.

2. In a bowl, combine carrot, bean sprouts, snow peas, mushrooms and cabbage. Add teriyaki sauce and toss until well combined. Serve immediately or cover and refrigerate for up to 2 days.

Variations

If you don't have Teriyaki Sauce on hand, substitute a mixture of 3 tbsp (45 mL) wheat-free tamari, 2 tbsp (30 mL) raw agave nectar, 2 tbsp (30 mL) sesame oil (untoasted) and 1 tbsp (15 mL) chopped gingerroot.

Coconut Curry Lo Mein: In Step 2, toss the vegetables with ½ cup (125 mL) Yellow Coconut Curry Sauce (page 22).

Jicama Pot Stickers

Jicama is a mildly sweet root vegetable that tastes like a blend of apple, potato and celery. Because of its high water content, it accepts flavor very well with marinating. When thinly sliced, it can also be manipulated into various shapes. In this dish jicama is stuffed with a rich "meaty" filling of ground walnuts and green onion.

Makes 3 to 4 servings

Tips

When purchasing jicama, look for it to be solid in color, uniform in shape and firm to the touch.

The jicama slices need to be thin enough to be pliable. If you cut them too thick they will break when you attempt to fold them. If the jicama is sliced thinly enough and marinated until soft, the edges should stick together when the slices are folded over the filling.

Walnuts provide alpha-linolenic acid (ALA), the omega-3 fat that is an essential fatty acid — without it, we could not survive. It is called "essential" because our bodies are unable to make it and we must obtain it from food. Research has demonstrated ALA's ability to reduce chronic inflammation and other risk factors for diabetes, heart disease and stroke.

- **Mandoline**

1	medium jicama, peeled (see Tips, left)	1
3 tbsp	freshly squeezed lemon juice	45 mL
$\frac{1}{4}$ tsp	fine sea salt	1 mL
2 cups	raw walnut halves	500 mL
$\frac{1}{4}$ cup	Teriyaki Sauce (page 22), divided	60 mL
$\frac{1}{4}$ cup	finely sliced green onion, green parts only, divided	60 mL

1. Using mandoline, slice jicama approximately $\frac{1}{16}$ inch (2 mm) thick (see Tips, left).

2. In a bowl, toss jicama, lemon juice and salt until well combined. Cover and set aside for 10 minutes, until softened.

3. In a food processor fitted with the metal blade, combine walnuts, 3 tbsp (45 mL) teriyaki sauce and 3 tbsp (45 mL) green onion. Process until very roughly chopped (be careful not to overprocess — you do not want to make a paste). Transfer to a bowl.

4. Lay jicama slices on a flat surface and place 1 tbsp (15 mL) walnut mixture in center of each slice. Using your fingers, fold each slice in half and gently pinch together edges to form a seal. Arrange finished pot stickers on a serving plate, drizzle with remaining teriyaki sauce and garnish with remaining green onion. Serve immediately or cover and refrigerate for up to 2 days.

Variations

You can substitute 1 medium beet, rutabaga or celery root for the jicama.

Main Courses

Many traditional main-course dishes include components such as meat and dairy. The main-course meals I have created for this book are distinguished by their raw ingredients. Nuts, seeds or mushrooms replace meat. These ingredients are paired with robust flavors such as wheat-free tamari or nutritional yeast, garlic and other aromatics, herbs and spices and cold-pressed oils. Vegetables are sliced, ground or shredded and are used as shells, wrappers and fillings. Creamy sauces are blended from ingredients such as raw cashews and tahini. While that may sound like a lot of work, main-course meals don't need to be complicated.

In this chapter I feature recipes that use five ingredients or less and are intended to be paired with other easy-to-prepare dishes in this book. For example, Stuffed Mushroom Caps (page 167) are delicious on their own, but paired with Creamed Garlic Spinach (page 181) or Cheesy Broccoli (page 185) they make a fantastic well-rounded meal. For an authentic-tasting Southwest meal, try pairing a Squash Burrito (page 159) with Cheesy Shoestring Jicama Fries (page 186) and Mexican Fiesta Dressing (page 27). Or top a Sweet Potato Enchilada (page 160) with Chunky Tomato Marinara Sauce (page 25) and Creamy Alfredo Sauce (page 24).

Some of the dishes in this chapter, such as Mushroom Tart (page 169) and Squash Burrito (page 159), are particularly satisfying because they create umami. *Umami*, which means "delicious flavor" in Japanese, describes a savory taste that is usually lacking in vegetarian cuisine. It is found in foods that contain glutamates, including some meats and cheese. Fortunately, certain vegetables — for instance, mushrooms and eggplant — can be flavored to create umami. When you marinate mushrooms in tamari, miso, olive oil and water, you imbue them with additional flavor and create a particularly pleasing mouth-feel. The end result helps you to feel satiated and content.

In raw cuisine it is important to understand how all the ingredients come together to create something that is greater than the sum of its parts. For example, finely chopped carrots stand in for rice in Maki Rolls with Carrot Rice and Avocado (page 156), and creamy cashews and cauliflower replace mashed potatoes in Shepherd's Pie (page 166). It is, after all, the art of combining ingredients that creates the unique and satisfying experience of enjoying a well-executed raw food meal.

Avocado Cucumber Hand Rolls

These hand rolls are refreshing, healthy and packed with protein. Serve them with Pickled Ginger (page 173) and a side of Asian Kale Slaw (page 120).

Makes 2 servings

Tips

To soak the sunflower seeds, place in a bowl and add 2 cups (500 mL) warm water. Cover and set aside for 10 minutes. Drain, discarding soaking water and any bits of shell or unwanted particles. Rinse under cold running water until the water runs clear.

Be sure to use high-quality nori that is labeled "raw." Purchase your nori from a reputable source such as your favorite raw foods retailer, health food store or well-stocked grocery store.

1 cup	raw sunflower seeds, soaked (see Tips, left)	250 mL
¼ cup	freshly squeezed lemon juice	60 mL
¼ cup	filtered water	60 mL
¼ tsp	fine sea salt	1 mL
1	sheet raw nori, cut in half lengthwise (see Tips, left)	1
½	medium cucumber, seeded and thinly sliced lengthwise	½
½	medium avocado, thinly sliced lengthwise	½

1. In a food processor fitted with the metal blade, process soaked sunflower seeds, lemon juice, water and salt until smooth.
2. Place 1 piece of nori, shiny side down, in the palm of your left hand (if you are right-handed), long edge facing you. Place half the sunflower mixture on a diagonal starting from the upper left corner. Top with half the cucumber and avocado slices. Fold bottom left corner of nori over filling and roll into a cone shape. Repeat with second piece of nori. Enjoy immediately.

Variations

Substitute an equal quantity of finely sliced red bell pepper for the cucumber.

For some added crunch, add 1 tsp (5 mL) raw white sesame seeds to each roll.

Maki Rolls with Carrot Rice and Avocado

One of the keys to successfully switching over to a diet high in raw foods is to mimic the flavors and textures that you are used to in your favorite foods. You'll be surprised at how similar the carrot in these rolls is to traditional sushi rice when it is processed and combined with vinegar and raw agave nectar.

Makes 2 servings

Tips

If you don't have a sushi mat, use a sheet of waxed paper. However, be aware that your maki rolls will not be as tight as when made using a sushi mat. It takes some time to get used to working with a sushi mat, but once you do, it is very simple.

Apple cider vinegar has long been used in folk medicine. It is a great digestive aid, among its other benefits. When purchasing apple cider vinegar, make sure it is raw, made from organically grown apples and contains the "mother," which is a source of healthy bacteria and enzymes.

I prefer to use organic sea salt. This type of salt is classified as a whole food and is said to contain many trace minerals. If salt intake is something you are concerned about, feel free to use less than called for or omit it completely.

- **Sushi mat, optional (see Tips, left)**

2 cups	finely chopped carrots	500 mL
2 tbsp	unpasteurized apple cider vinegar (see Tips, left)	30 mL
1 tbsp	raw agave nectar	15 mL
1/2 tsp	fine sea salt	2 mL
1/2	medium avocado, thinly sliced lengthwise	1/2
2	sheets raw nori (see Tip, page 157)	2

1. In a food processor fitted with the metal blade, process carrots just until rice-like in consistency (be careful not to overprocess or they will become soft and mushy).

2. In a bowl, combine processed carrots, vinegar, agave nectar and salt. Mix well.

3. Place sushi mat on a flat surface with bamboo strips running crosswise. Place 1 sheet nori on mat, shiny side down. Spread half the carrot mixture over nori, pressing it out until it is about $1/4$ inch (0.5 cm) thick, leaving a border of $1 1/2$ inches (4 cm) along the edge farthest away from you. Place half the avocado slices on top in a crosswise row about $1/2$ inch (1 cm) from the closest edge.

4. Place your thumb underneath sushi mat and index finger on top. Using your remaining fingers to hold filling in place, gently roll nori with mat, tucking in edges as you roll, to make a cylinder shape. Continue to roll sushi, taking care to tuck in nori — but not the mat itself — as you roll. Using both hands, grab mat and roll it a few times to tighten. Repeat several times during rolling process to make sushi as tight as possible.

Tip

Be sure to use high-quality nori that is labeled "raw." Purchase your nori from a reputable source such as your favorite raw foods retailer, health food store or well-stocked grocery store.

5. Once you have rolled all the way to the top, wet your finger with a little water and lightly moisten free top edge of nori. Make one final roll to seal edge. Remove mat and cut cylinder crosswise into 8 equal slices. Repeat with second nori sheet. If not serving immediately, leave roll whole (do not cut) and cover and refrigerate for up to 2 days.

Kale Spring Rolls

These delicious spring rolls are perfect for busy days when you don't have much time to eat. Make them ahead so you can pack them for a quick meal on the go.

Makes 4 rolls

Tips

If the stems of the kale leaves are thick, remove them with a small paring knife.

Hemp seeds are considered a complete protein, meaning that they contain all eight essential amino acids. One tablespoon (15 mL) raw shelled hemp seeds provides up to 5 grams of protein and appreciable amounts of vitamins B_1 (thiamine) and B_6 (pyridoxine), folate, phosphorus, magnesium, zinc and manganese. Two tablespoons (30 mL) hemp seeds meets your daily requirement for omega-3 essential fatty acids.

4	large leaves black kale, trimmed (see Tips, left)	4
¼ cup	freshly squeezed lemon juice, divided	60 mL
½ tsp	fine sea salt, divided	2 mL
1 cup	shredded carrots	250 mL
1 cup	shredded beets	250 mL
½ cup	raw shelled hemp seeds	125 mL

1. In a bowl, combine kale, 2 tbsp (30 mL) lemon juice and ⅛ tsp (0.5 mL) salt. Toss until well combined. Cover and set aside for 5 minutes, until softened.

2. In another bowl, combine carrots, beets, hemp seeds and remaining lemon juice and salt. Toss until well combined. Cover and set aside for 5 minutes, until softened.

3. Remove kale from marinade, pat each leaf dry and place on a flat surface. Discard marinade. Divide carrot-beet filling into 4 equal portions. Place one portion on the bottom third of each kale leaf. Starting at the bottom of the leaf, roll up around the filling, making a tight cylinder. Transfer to a serving dish. Serve immediately or cover and refrigerate for up to 2 days.

Variations

Substitute 4 large collard or Swiss chard leaves for the kale leaves.

For creamy rolls, in Step 2, toss the shredded carrots and beets with ½ cup (125 mL) Quick Thai Cream Sauce (page 23) or ¼ cup (60 mL) Creamy Alfredo Sauce (page 24).

Squash Burrito

Burritos traditionally use wraps made from wheat flour, which contains gluten, a type of protein that creates digestive problems for many people. This burrito is wrapped in thinly shaved butternut squash, making it mildly sweet, with a crunchy texture.

Makes 1 serving

Tip

To cube the avocado for this recipe, cut it in half and remove the pit. Using a paring knife, make incisions in the flesh from top to bottom. Turn the avocado 90 degrees and make incisions in the flesh in the opposite direction. Turn the skin inside out and gently push out the cubed flesh.

1	medium butternut squash, peeled, top part only	1
3 tbsp	freshly squeezed lemon juice, divided	45 mL
$\frac{1}{2}$ tsp	fine sea salt, divided	2 mL
$\frac{1}{2}$	medium avocado, cubed (see Tip, left)	$\frac{1}{2}$
$\frac{1}{4}$ cup	chopped tomato	60 mL
$\frac{1}{2}$ cup	Sunflower Seed Hummus (page 29)	125 mL

1. Over a bowl, using a vegetable peeler, peel the squash lengthwise into long, thin strips. Add 2 tbsp (30 mL) lemon juice and $\frac{1}{4}$ tsp (1 mL) salt and toss well. Cover and set aside for 10 minutes, until softened.

2. In another bowl, combine avocado, tomato and remaining lemon juice and salt. Toss until well combined. Set aside.

3. Remove squash from marinade and pat dry. On a flat surface, lay strips vertically so that each overlaps the next by $\frac{1}{2}$ inch (1 cm); the row of strips should be approximately 6 inches (15 cm) long. Spread hummus and tomato-avocado mixture across middle of row. Starting at bottom of the strips, roll them up together around the filling, making a cylinder. Place seam side down on a serving plate. Serve immediately or cover and refrigerate for up to 2 days.

Variation

Substitute 1 large peeled sweet potato for the squash.

Sweet Potato Enchilada

In this dish, thin strips of sweet potato stuffed with creamy Sunflower Seed Hummus stand in for ground meat deep-fried in a corn tortilla. Top with Chunky Tomato Marinara Sauce and this take on a Mexican classic is sure to become a trusted favorite.

Makes 2 servings

Tips

To soak the cashews, place in a bowl and cover with 1 cup (250 mL) warm water. Cover and set aside for 10 minutes. Drain, discarding soaking water, and rinse under cold running water until the water runs clear.

Typically a medium-sized lemon will yield about 3 tbsp (45 mL) fresh lemon juice.

Raw sweet potato is dense and rather starchy. To help give it a pleasant mouth-feel, be sure to slice it thinly and soften in a marinade that contains some form of acid, such as the lemon juice used in this recipe.

- **Mandoline**

$1/2$ cup	whole raw cashews, soaked (see Tips, left)	125 mL
1	medium sweet potato, peeled	1
3 tbsp	freshly squeezed lemon juice, divided	45 mL
$1/2$ tsp	fine sea salt, divided	2 mL
$1^1/2$ cups	Sunflower Seed Hummus (page 29)	375 mL
$1/2$ cup	Chunky Tomato Marinara Sauce (page 25)	125 mL

1. Using mandoline, slice sweet potato lengthwise into 6 strips approximately $1/8$ inch (3 mm) thick. In a bowl, toss strips with 2 tbsp (30 mL) lemon juice and $1/4$ tsp (1 mL) salt until well coated. Cover and set aside for 10 minutes, until softened.

2. In a blender, combine cashews, water, 1 tbsp (15 mL) lemon juice and remaining $1/4$ tsp (1 mL) salt. Blend at high speed until smooth. Set aside.

3. Remove sweet potato from marinade and pat dry. Lay slices on a flat surface and place $1/4$ cup (60 mL) Sunflower Seed Hummus on bottom third of each slice. Starting at the bottom, roll each up into a cylinder. Arrange seam side down on two serving plates. Top each serving with $1/4$ cup (60 mL) marinara sauce and 2 tbsp (30 mL) of the cashew mixture from Step 2. Serve immediately or cover and refrigerate for up to 2 days.

Avocado Cucumber Hand Rolls (page 155)

Squash Burrito (page 159)

Lime, Tomato and Avocado Chili (page 161)

Summer Corn Cakes (page 162)

Curried Cashews and Mixed Vegetables (page 164)

Mushroom Tart (page 169)

Stuffed Cucumber Cups (page 174)

Strawberry Coconut Shortcake Tart (page 203)

Mini Chocolate Banana Flax Cakes (page 205)

Lime, Tomato and Avocado Chili

You will love the mildly spicy flavor of this rich, warming dish. The ground walnuts provide protein and will leave you feeling satisfied. Serve this chili with a Squash Burrito (page 159) and a side of Mexican Jicama Slaw (page 123).

Makes 2 servings

Tips

To soak the sun-dried tomatoes, place in a bowl with 2 cups (500 mL) warm water. Cover and set aside for 12 minutes. Drain, discarding soaking liquid.

Be sure to use ripe avocado. To ripen, place in a brown paper bag with a tomato or an apple. If your avocado is ripe and won't be consumed within a day or two, place it in the coolest part of the refrigerator to lengthen its life by three to four days. Once you take an avocado out of the fridge, do not put it back in or it will turn black.

½ cup	sun-dried tomatoes, soaked (see Tips, left)	125 mL
¾ cup	warm water	175 mL
1	medium avocado (see Tips, left)	1
¼ cup	freshly squeezed lime juice	60 mL
1 tbsp	chili powder	15 mL
¼ tsp	fine sea salt	1 mL
½ cup	Spiced Nut Crumble (page 30 or Variation, below)	125 mL

1. In a food processor fitted with the metal blade, process soaked sun-dried tomatoes and water until smooth. Add avocado, lime juice, chili powder and salt and process until smooth. Transfer to a bowl and stir in nut crumble. Serve immediately or cover and refrigerate for up to 2 days.

Variation

If you don't have Spiced Nut Crumble on hand, use this substitute which makes a quantity appropriate for this recipe: In a food processor fitted with the metal blade, combine 1 cup (250 mL) raw walnut halves, 1 tbsp (15 mL) extra virgin olive oil, 1 tbsp (15 mL) wheat-free tamari and 1 tsp (5 mL) ground cumin. Process until roughly chopped and the mixture begins to stick together.

Summer Corn Cakes

Serve these sweet, light cakes with something creamy such as Zucchini Fettuccini Alfredo (page 145) or with a crisp salad such as Mexican Jicama Slaw (page 123).

Makes 4 servings

Tips

To yield the maximum juice from citrus fruits, allow them to sit at room temperature for 30 minutes before juicing. Once the fruit is at room temperature, use the palm of your hand to roll it on the counter to release the juices before slicing and squeezing.

Use either golden or brown flax seeds for this recipe. Golden flax seeds will make the cakes lighter in color while brown flax will make them darker.

2 cups	fresh corn kernels	500 mL
2 tbsp	filtered water	30 mL
2 tbsp	freshly squeezed lemon juice	30 mL
1 tbsp	chopped fresh thyme leaves	15 mL
1/2 tsp	fine sea salt	2 mL
1/2 cup	finely diced red bell pepper	125 mL
1 cup	ground flax seeds (see Tips, left)	250 mL

1. In a food processor fitted with the metal blade, combine corn, water, lemon juice, thyme and salt. Process until smooth. Transfer to a bowl.

2. Add red pepper and ground flax seeds. Mix well. Cover and set aside for 10 minutes to allow the flax to absorb some of the liquid and swell.

3. Using a 1/4-cup (60 mL) measure, divide mixture into 4 equal portions and, using your hands, shape into round cakes. Transfer to a serving plate. Serve immediately or cover and refrigerate for up to 3 days.

Variation

If you enjoy spice, add 1/2 tsp (2 mL) chili powder and 1/4 tsp (1 mL) smoked paprika in Step 1.

Julienne "Stir-Fry"

This light, crisp vegetable medley tossed with tangy teriyaki sauce is delicious served on its own or paired with Deep-Sea Seaweed (page 180) and some spicy Pickled Ginger (page 173).

Makes 2 servings

Tips

You can substitute green, yellow or orange bell peppers for the red peppers.

The outer stalks of celery can be tough and fibrous. For best results, peel the stalk with a vegetable peeler prior to cutting. Removing the skin will soften the celery and make it easier to consume raw.

1 cup	finely sliced red bell peppers (see Tips, left)	250 mL
½ cup	finely sliced celery (see Tips, left)	125 mL
½ cup	shredded carrot	125 mL
¼ cup	Teriyaki Sauce (page 22)	60 mL
3 tbsp	raw shelled hemp seeds	45 mL

1. In a bowl, toss red peppers, celery, carrot, teriyaki sauce and hemp seeds until well combined. Cover and set aside for 10 minutes, until softened. Serve immediately or cover and refrigerate for up to 2 days.

Variation

I like to garnish this recipe with 1 tsp (5 mL) raw sesame seeds.

Curried Cashews and Mixed Vegetables

This rich medley of crunchy cashews and fresh vegetables with aromatic seasoning is a wonderful dinner entrée. Serve this with a simple green salad.

Makes 1 serving

Tips

Try substituting an equal amount of thinly sliced leafy greens, such as spinach, kale, dandelion greens or mustard greens, in place of the broccoli.

I prefer to use organic sea salt. This type of salt is classified as a whole food and is said to contain many trace minerals. If salt intake is something you are concerned about, feel free to use less than called for or omit it completely.

1½ cups	whole raw cashews, divided	375 mL
½ cup	filtered water	125 mL
2 tbsp	freshly squeezed lemon juice, divided	30 mL
2 tsp	curry powder	10 mL
½ tsp	fine sea salt, divided	2 mL
½ cup	broccoli florets cut into ½-inch (1 cm) pieces (see Tips, left)	125 mL
½ cup	shredded carrot	125 mL

1. In a blender, combine 1 cup (250 mL) cashews, water, 1 tbsp (15 mL) lemon juice, curry powder and ¼ tsp (1 mL) salt. Blend at high speed until smooth. Cover and set aside.

2. In a bowl, combine broccoli and carrot. Add remaining salt and lemon juice and toss until well combined. Cover and set aside for 10 minutes, until softened.

3. Add remaining whole cashews and cashew curry sauce to softened vegetables. Toss until well combined. Serve immediately or cover and refrigerate for up to 2 days.

Variations

Replace the curry powder with an equal amount of garam masala and the broccoli with an equal amount of cauliflower.

I often add 2 tsp (10 mL) finely grated gingerroot to the vegetables in Step 3.

Vegetable "Fried Rice"

You will love how much this dish tastes like Chinese takeout — without any of the hidden ingredients. Serve with Sweet-and-Sour Kale (page 179), Deep-Sea Seaweed (page 180) or Pickled Ginger (page 173).

Serve with Sweet-and-Sour Kale (page 179), Deep-Sea Seaweed (page 180) or Pickled Ginger (page 173).

Makes 2 servings

Tips

When pulsing the cauliflower, be sure not to overprocess — otherwise the cell walls of the cauliflower will break down and the "rice" will become soggy. You want the texture to be light and fluffy.

To remove the skin from a clove of garlic, use the butt end of a chef's knife to press firmly but gently on the clove to loosen the skin. Using your index finger and thumb, carefully ease off the skin.

4 cups	chopped cauliflower florets	1 L
1/4 cup	Teriyaki Sauce (page 22)	60 mL
2 tbsp	chopped gingerroot	30 mL
2	cloves garlic (see Tips, left)	2
2 tbsp	finely sliced green onion, green part only	30 mL

1. In a food processor fitted with the metal blade, process cauliflower until it breaks down into a rice-like consistency, pulsing 10 to 15 times (see Tips, left). Transfer to a bowl and set aside.
2. In same work bowl, combine teriyaki sauce, ginger and garlic. Process until smooth.
3. Add sauce mixture and green onion to processed cauliflower. Mix well. Serve immediately or cover and refrigerate for up to 2 days.

Variations

Substitute an equal amount of chopped peeled parsnip or jicama for the cauliflower in Step 1. Once the jicama has been processed, place it in a fine-mesh sieve or cheesecloth and, using the back of a blade, press to remove excess water.

I like to garnish this dish with 3 tbsp (45 mL) raw sesame seeds and 2 tbsp (30 mL) raw shelled hemp seeds.

Shepherd's Pie

You are sure to enjoy this creamy blend of cauliflower "mashed potatoes" and fresh vegetables with ground walnuts. It takes a bit of extra effort to prepare, but you'll find it's well worth it. Serve with a crisp green salad tossed with Easy Italian Dressing (page 127).

Makes 2 to 3 servings

Tip

To remove kernels from a cob of corn, cut pieces from the top and bottom of the cob to create flat surfaces. Stand up the cob on a flat end. Using a chef's knife in a downward motion, gently strip away the kernels, making sure not to remove too much of the starchy white body of the cob.

- **6-inch (15 cm) square glass baking dish**

½ cup	finely chopped carrot	125 mL
¼ cup	finely chopped celery	60 mL
3 tbsp	filtered water	45 mL
¼ tsp	fine sea salt	1 mL
1 cup	fresh corn kernels (see Tip, left)	250 mL
½ cup	Spiced Nut Crumble (page 30)	125 mL
1 cup	Cauliflower "Mashed Potatoes" (page 21)	250 mL

1. In a food processor fitted with the metal blade, process carrot, celery, water and salt until roughly chopped (you want to retain some texture). Add corn and pulse 3 or 4 times to combine. Add Spiced Nut Crumble and pulse 2 to 3 times to combine.

2. Transfer to baking dish and spread evenly. Top with cauliflower "mashed potatoes." Serve immediately or cover and refrigerate for up to 3 days.

Stuffed Mushroom Caps

These stuffed mushrooms are rich and meaty. Serve with Red Pepper and Hemp Purée (page 175) and some Cheesy Broccoli (page 185) for a perfectly balanced meal.

Makes 2 servings

Tips

This recipe works best with large button mushrooms. If you use smaller ones, reduce the amount of stuffing to 1 to 2 tsp (5 to 10 mL) per mushroom.

You can use portobello mushrooms but you will need to marinate them longer, for 20 to 30 minutes or until softened. To speed up the marinating time, you can remove the gills. To do this, use the edge of a teaspoon to gently scrape away the dark gills on the underside of the mushroom.

2 cups	large button mushrooms, stems removed (see Tips, left)	500 mL
¼ cup	cold-pressed (extra virgin) olive oil	60 mL
3 tbsp	wheat-free tamari	45 mL
1 tbsp	chopped fresh thyme leaves	15 mL
½ cup	Sunflower Seed Hummus (page 29)	125 mL

1. In a bowl, combine mushrooms, olive oil, tamari and thyme. Toss until well coated. Cover and set aside for 15 minutes or until softened.
2. Remove mushrooms from marinade and pat dry. Discard marinade. Lay mushrooms, gill side up, on a serving platter. Using a spoon, place 1 to 2 tbsp (15 to 30 mL) hummus in center of each mushroom. Serve immediately or cover and refrigerate for up to 3 days.

Variation

Chunky Sunflower-Stuffed Mushrooms: Replace the hummus with 1 cup (250 mL) sunflower seeds, ¼ cup (60 mL) freshly squeezed lemon juice, ¼ cup (60 mL) filtered water, ¼ tsp (1 mL) fine sea salt and 1 clove garlic. Combine the ingredients in a food processor fitted with the metal blade and pulse until smooth.

Mushroom "Fricassee"

The unique meaty texture of the oyster and shiitake mushrooms in this dish is a wonderful complement to Celery Root Ravioli (page 147), Jicama Pot Stickers (page 152) or Crunchy Cabbage and Carrot Slaw (page 122).

Makes 2 servings

Tips

To prepare the oyster mushrooms, trim and discard the tough, fibrous end of the stems, then use your fingers to gently tear them into strips approximately 1/4 inch (0.5 cm) wide.

You can substitute an equal amount of exotic mushrooms such as chanterelles for the oyster mushrooms in this recipe.

To clean mushrooms, use a damp cloth to brush off any dirt from the surface. Never clean mushrooms with water. They are like sponges — they will absorb the water and turn gray.

2 cups	oyster mushrooms (see Tips, left)	500 mL
1 cup	finely sliced shiitake mushrooms	250 mL
3 tbsp	wheat-free tamari	45 mL
3 tbsp	cold-pressed (extra virgin) olive oil	45 mL
1 tbsp	chopped fresh thyme leaves	15 mL

1. In a bowl, toss oyster and shiitake mushrooms, tamari, olive oil and thyme until well combined. Cover and set aside for 15 minutes, until softened. Serve immediately or cover and refrigerate for up to 5 days.

Mushroom Tart

This tart's dense shell and creamy mushroom filling will be sure to fulfill your cravings for something hearty and rich. Serve this with Red Pepper and Hemp Purée (page 175) and Exotic Cauliflower (page 178).

(page 175)(page 178)

Makes 2 servings

Tips

Substitute an equal amount of thinly sliced shiitake mushrooms, stems removed, for the button mushrooms.

While wheat-free tamari is not raw, it is gluten-free. The raw alternative for tamari, nama shoyu, does contain gluten. If you are following a completely raw diet and can tolerate gluten, by all means substitute an equal quantity of nama shoyu.

Although extra virgin olive oil should, by definition, be cold-pressed, it is worth checking the label. Some olive oils are extracted using a centrifuge system, which spins the olives at a very high rate. This heats the olives and the resulting oil, depriving it of its raw status.

- **Two 4-inch (10 cm) quiche molds, lined with plastic wrap**

4 cups	thinly sliced button mushrooms (see Tips, left)	1 L
¼ cup	wheat-free tamari (see Tips, left)	60 mL
2 tbsp	cold-pressed (extra virgin) olive oil (see Tips, left)	30 mL
1 cup	whole raw almonds	250 mL
¼ tsp	fine sea salt	1 mL
6 tbsp	filtered water, divided	90 mL
1 cup	whole raw cashews	250 mL

1. In a bowl, toss mushrooms, tamari and olive oil until well combined. Cover and set aside for 10 minutes, until softened.
2. In a food processor fitted with the metal blade, combine almonds and salt and process until flour-like in consistency. Transfer to a bowl. Add 3 tbsp (45 mL) water and mix well. Divide mixture into 2 equal parts and press into prepared quiche molds.
3. In food processor, combine marinated mushrooms, remaining water and cashews. Process until smooth, stopping motor to scrape down sides of work bowl as necessary. Divide mixture in half and spread in each prepared crust. Serve immediately or cover and refrigerate for up to 2 days.

Variation

Add ½ cup (125 mL) baby spinach, 2 tbsp (30 mL) nutritional yeast and 1 tbsp (15 mL) chopped fresh thyme to the food processor in Step 3.

"Steak and Potatoes"

This is a comforting recipe for when you're craving something hearty and rich. The thinly sliced meaty portobello mushrooms and blended almonds make a perfect pairing with Cheesy Shoestring Jicama Fries (page 186) and Cheesy Broccoli (page 185).

Makes 2 servings

Tips

To slice the mushrooms, use a sharp chef's knife and cut them on a slight bias. You want to expose as much surface area as possible so the marinade can penetrate the mushrooms and soften them.

While wheat-free tamari is not raw, it is gluten-free. The raw alternative for tamari, nama shoyu, does contain gluten. If you are following a completely raw diet and can tolerate gluten, by all means substitute an equal amount of nama shoyu.

When purchasing nuts, be sure to look for products labeled "raw." Most of the nuts on the market have been roasted and do not qualify as raw food. If you have concerns, ask your purveyor.

2	medium portobello mushrooms, thinly sliced (see Tips, left)	2
¼ cup	cold-pressed (extra virgin) olive oil	60 mL
3 tbsp	wheat-free tamari (see Tips, left)	45 mL
1½ cups	whole raw almonds	375 mL
2 tbsp	nutritional yeast	30 mL
¼ tsp	fine sea salt	1 mL
½ cup	filtered water	125 mL

1. In a bowl, toss mushrooms with olive oil and tamari, until well coated. Cover and set aside for 12 to 13 minutes, until softened.

2. In a food processor fitted with the metal blade, process almonds, nutritional yeast and salt until combined and no large pieces remain. With the motor running, slowly drizzle water through the feed tube to create a paste. Process for 20 to 30 seconds.

3. Transfer almond mixture to a blender. Blend at high speed until smooth and creamy, stopping motor to scrape down sides of jar as necessary.

4. Place almond mixture in the middle of a serving plate and top with marinated mushrooms. Serve immediately or cover and refrigerate for up to 3 days.

Variation

If you have more time, try replacing the almond mixture (Step 2) in this recipe with 1 cup (250 mL) Cauliflower "Mashed Potatoes" (page 21).

Sides

In raw food cuisine a meal is often a collection of several small plates rather than one large main course. This chapter focuses on dishes that work best as smaller portions and are best paired with other recipes found in this book. For example, Red Pepper and Hemp Purée (page 175) is a wonderful addition to a main-course dish such as Summer Corn Cakes (page 162), Sweet Potato Enchilada (page 160) or Mushroom "Fricassee" (page 168). A simple side of Pickled Ginger (page 173) is the perfect complement to Asian-inspired dishes such as Maki Rolls with Carrot Rice and Avocado (page 156) and Avocado Cucumber Hand Rolls (page 155).

Other sides, such as Cheesy Broccoli (page 185) and Sweet-and-Sour Kale (page 179), make a great meal on their own when doubled or tripled in size. There are many different ways to use the recipes in this chapter. By experimenting, you will find what works best for you.

Pickled Ginger

The spiciness of raw pickled ginger packs a real flavor punch, especially when served with Asian-influenced dishes such as Avocado Cucumber Hand Rolls (page 155), Julienne "Stir-Fry" (page 163) or Maki Rolls with Carrot Rice and Avocado (page 156).

Makes 4 side servings

Tips

Use a mandoline to slice the ginger about $\frac{1}{16}$ inch (2 mm) thick.

I like to triple this recipe and keep it in the fridge so I have it on hand any time I want to add fresh ginger to a dish.

6 tbsp	unpasteurized apple cider vinegar (see Tips, page 179)	90 mL
¼ cup	filtered water	60 mL
¼ cup	raw agave nectar	60 mL
¼ tsp	fine sea salt	1 mL
¼ cup	thinly sliced peeled gingerroot (see Tips, page 180)	60 mL

1. In a bowl, whisk together vinegar, water, agave nectar and salt. Add ginger and stir to combine. Cover and set aside for 10 minutes, until softened. Serve immediately or cover and refrigerate for up to 2 weeks.

Marinated Chia Olives

A twist on Italian marinated olives, these include chia seeds, which add a slight crunch as well as protein and healthy fats. I like to serve these as a side with Caprese Stacked Salad (page 112) or Spaghetti and Seed Balls (page 143).

Makes 2 side servings

Tips

You can use either white or black chia seeds for this recipe.

Two tablespoons (30 mL) chia seeds provides about 7 grams of alpha-linolenic acid (ALA), an omega-3 fat that is an essential fatty acid — without it, we could not survive. It is called "essential" because our bodies are unable to make it and must obtain it from food. Good sources of ALA include flax seeds, chia seeds and walnuts.

1 cup	green olives	250 mL
2 tbsp	chia seeds (see Tips, left)	30 mL
2 tbsp	cold-pressed (extra virgin) olive oil	30 mL
1 tbsp	lemon zest	15 mL
2 tsp	freshly squeezed lemon juice	10 mL

1. In a bowl, toss olives, chia seeds, olive oil, and lemon zest and juice until well combined. Serve immediately or cover and refrigerate for up to 5 days.

Variation

Herbed Marinated Chia Olives: Add ½ cup (125 mL) roughly chopped flat-leaf (Italian) parsley leaves, 1 tbsp (15 mL) chopped fresh thyme leaves and 1 tsp (5 mL) chopped fresh rosemary.

Stuffed Cucumber Cups

These little stuffed cups balance the slightly sweet taste and creamy texture of cashews with fresh cucumber. Try serving them with a simple salad of crisp romaine lettuce drizzled with Smoked Paprika and Red Pepper Dressing (page 134).

¾ cup	whole raw cashews	175 mL
½ cup	chopped red bell pepper	125 mL
¼ cup	filtered water	60 mL
2 tbsp	freshly squeezed lemon juice (see Tips, left)	30 mL
2 tsp	smoked paprika	10 mL
¾ tsp	fine sea salt	3 mL
1	clove garlic	1
1	large cucumber (see Tips, left)	1

Makes 10 to 12 pieces

Tips

If you can, use an English cucumber to make the cups, as they do not contain seeds. If you are using a field cucumber, be sure to peel off the skin and scoop out all the seeds — they are tough and bitter.

Cashews provide protein, copper, zinc, phosphorus, potassium and magnesium as well as healthy monounsaturated fat.

Typically a medium-sized lemon will yield about 3 tbsp (45 mL) fresh lemon juice.

1. In a food processor fitted with the metal blade, combine cashews, red pepper, water, lemon juice, paprika, salt and garlic. Process until smooth. Transfer to a bowl and set aside.

2. Cut the ends off the cucumber, then cut it crosswise into 10 to 12 equal pieces. Using a melon baller, scoop out the seeds and pulp from each piece, hollowing it out to make a ring.

3. Place the cucumber cups on a serving plate. Fill each with 1 tbsp (15 mL) of the cashew mixture. Serve immediately or cover and refrigerate for up to 2 days.

Variations

Try stuffing the cucumber cups with an equal amount of Sunflower Seed Hummus (page 29), Herbed Cashew Cheese (page 20) or Tahini Tzatziki (page 28).

Red Pepper and Hemp Purée

The hemp seeds in this purée not only add protein but also create a rich, creamy texture that marries well with sweet red pepper. I like to use it as a base or sauce for Shepherd's Pie (page 166), Cheesy Broccoli (page 185) and Kale Spring Rolls (page 158).

Makes
½ cup (125 mL)

Tips

You may substitute an equal amount of yellow bell pepper for the red one.

To soak the hemp seeds, place in a bowl and add 1 cup (250 mL) water. Cover and set aside for 20 minutes. Drain, discarding soaking water. Rinse under cold running water until the water runs clear.

Typically a medium-sized lemon will yield about 3 tbsp (45 mL) fresh lemon juice.

I prefer to use organic sea salt. This type of salt is classified as a whole food and is said to contain many trace minerals. If salt intake is something you are concerned about, feel free to use less than called for or omit it completely.

1 cup	chopped red bell pepper (see Tips, left)	250 mL
½ cup	raw shelled hemp seeds, soaked (see Tips, left)	125 mL
3 tbsp	filtered water	45 mL
3 tbsp	cold-pressed (extra virgin) olive oil	45 mL
2 tbsp	freshly squeezed lemon juice (see Tips, left)	30 mL
½ tsp	fine sea salt	2 mL

1. In a blender, combine red pepper, soaked hemp seeds, water, olive oil, lemon juice and salt. Blend at high speed until smooth. Transfer to a bowl. Serve immediately or cover and refrigerate for up to 2 days.

Variations

Add your favorite dried herb or spice to this recipe. Try ½ tsp (2 mL) chili powder, ground cumin, smoked paprika, dried dill weed, dried oregano or dried basil.

Avocado and Olive Relish

In this pleasing relish, salty olives help to provide a great mouth-feel and are balanced by rich and creamy avocado. Serve this with Mushroom Tart (page 169) or "Steak and Potatoes" (page 170).

**Makes
4 side servings**

Tips

For this recipe, try to use an avocado that is ripe but firm. This will make it easier to dice into small pieces without crushing it.

To ripen avocados, place them in a brown paper bag with a tomato or apple. If your avocado is ripe and won't be consumed within a day or two, place it in the coolest part of the refrigerator to lengthen its life by three to four days. Once you take an avocado out of the fridge, do not put it back in, or it will turn black.

I like to use kalamata olives for this recipe, but feel free to substitute any type of olive in the same quantity.

1 cup	finely diced avocado (see Tips, left)	250 mL
¼ cup	finely chopped kalamata olives (see Tips, left)	60 mL
3 tbsp	raw agave nectar	45 mL
2 tbsp	unpasteurized apple cider vinegar (see Tips, page 179)	30 mL
1 tsp	freshly squeezed lemon juice	5 mL

1. In a bowl, toss avocado, olives, agave nectar, vinegar and lemon juice until well combined. Serve immediately or cover and refrigerate for up to 2 days.

Variation

Substitute an equal amount of fresh lime juice for the lemon juice.

Avocado Corn Salsa

You'll love this fresh combination of juicy sweet corn and rich, creamy avocado. Serve this salsa with Summer Corn Cakes (page 162), Squash Burrito (page 159) or Stuffed Mushroom Caps (page 167).

**Makes
2 side servings**

Tips

Cut the avocado into cubes about 1/2 inch (1 cm) in size. To cube the avocado, cut it in half and remove the pit. Using a paring knife, make incisions in the flesh from top to bottom. Turn the avocado 90 degrees and make incisions in the flesh in the opposite direction. Turn the skin inside out and gently push out the cubed flesh.

Although extra virgin olive oil should, by definition, be cold-pressed, it is worth checking the label. Some olive oils are extracted using a centrifuge system, which spins the olives at a very high rate. This heats the olives and the resulting oil, depriving it of its raw status.

1 cup	cubed avocado (see Tips, left)	250 mL
1/2 cup	fresh corn kernels	125 mL
1/4 cup	cold-pressed (extra virgin) olive oil (see Tips, left)	60 mL
3 tbsp	freshly squeezed lemon juice	45 mL
1/4 cup	finely diced red onion	60 mL
1/2 tsp	fine sea salt	2 mL

1. In a bowl, toss avocado, corn, olive oil, lemon juice, onion and salt until well combined. Serve immediately or cover and refrigerate for up to 1 day.

Variations

You can substitute an equal amount fresh lime juice for the lemon juice.

Try adding 1/2 cup (125 mL) roughly chopped fresh cilantro and a pinch of cayenne pepper.

Exotic Cauliflower

I love the versatility of raw cauliflower and its different textures. In this dish it's both crunchy and smooth, and the combination of aromatic turmeric and rich chili powder gives it a unique flavor reminiscent of Indian cuisine.

Makes 4 side servings

Tips

Cut the cauliflower into florets approximately 1/4 inch (0.5 cm) in diameter so the ingredients can penetrate and soften it.

Nutritional yeast flakes can be found in well-stocked supermarkets and natural foods stores. Although not a raw product, nutritional yeast is fortified with vitamin B_{12} and helps to produce umami, the savory flavor sometimes lacking in vegetarian cuisine.

I prefer to use organic sea salt. This type of salt is classified as a whole food and is said to contain many trace minerals. If salt intake is something you are concerned about, feel free to use less than called for or omit it completely.

3 cups	cauliflower florets, divided (see Tips, left)	750 mL
1/4 cup	filtered water	60 mL
1/4 cup	nutritional yeast (see Tips, left)	60 mL
3 tbsp	cold-pressed (extra virgin) olive oil, divided	45 mL
1/2 tsp	fine sea salt, divided (see Tips, left)	2 mL
1/4 tsp	ground turmeric	1 mL
1/2 tsp	chili powder	2 mL

1. In a blender, combine 1 cup (250 mL) cauliflower florets, water, nutritional yeast, 2 tbsp (30 mL) olive oil, 1/4 tsp (1 mL) salt and turmeric. Blend at high speed until smooth.

2. In a bowl, combine remaining cauliflower, olive oil and salt, chili powder and cauliflower purée. Mix well. Serve immediately or cover and refrigerate for up to 2 days.

Variation

To make this dish even creamier, add 1/4 cup (60 mL) whole raw cashews to the blender in Step 1.

Sweet-and-Sour Kale

I love how easily kale can be incorporated into Asian-inspired dishes. Try this with Avocado Cucumber Hand Rolls (page 155) or Julienne "Stir-Fry" (page 163). You'll enjoy this rich and savory side dish so much you'll turn to it as a midday snack as well.

**Makes
4 side servings**

Tips

Green kale is bulkier and has a higher water content than black kale. If using black kale, increase the quantity to 6 cups (1.5 L).

Before slicing the kale, remove the long stem that runs up through the leaf almost to the top of the plant. Use only the leafy green parts.

Apple cider vinegar has long been used in folk medicine. It is a great digestive aid, among its other benefits. When purchasing apple cider vinegar, make sure it is raw, made from organically grown apples and contains the "mother," which is a source of healthy bacteria and enzymes.

4 cups	finely sliced trimmed kale (see Tips, left)	1 L
½ cup	finely sliced red bell pepper	125 mL
¼ cup	cold-pressed (extra virgin) olive oil	60 mL
3 tbsp	unpasteurized apple cider vinegar (see Tips, left)	45 mL
½ tsp	fine sea salt	2 mL
¼ cup	raw agave nectar	60 mL

1. In a bowl, combine kale, red pepper, olive oil, vinegar and salt. Cover and set aside for 10 minutes, until softened. Add agave nectar and toss to combine. Serve immediately or cover and refrigerate for up to 2 days.

Variation

Substitute an equal amount of finely sliced baby bok choy for the kale.

Deep-Sea Seaweed

Its rich combination of tamari, vinegar and agave nectar will make this a dish you return to repeatedly. Serve it with Kale Spring Rolls (page 158), Maki Rolls with Carrot Rice and Avocado (page 156) or Julienne "Stir-Fry" (page 153).

**Makes
2 side servings**

Tips

To soak the arame, place in a bowl with 1¾ cups (425 mL) hot water. Cover and set aside for 12 minutes, until softened. Drain, discarding soaking liquid.

To remove the skin from fresh gingerroot with the least amount of waste, use the edge of a teaspoon. With a brushing motion, scrape off the skin to reveal the yellow root.

1 cup	arame, soaked (see Tips, left)	250 mL
¼ cup	hot water	60 mL
3 tbsp	wheat-free tamari	45 mL
2 tbsp	unpasteurized apple cider vinegar (see Tips, left)	30 mL
2 tbsp	raw agave nectar	30 mL
1 tbsp	chopped gingerroot (see Tips, left)	15 mL

1. In a blender, combine water, tamari, vinegar, agave nectar and ginger. Blend at high speed until smooth.
2. In a bowl, toss soaked arame with the dressing until well coated. Serve immediately or cover and refrigerate for up to 3 days.

Variations

Substitute an equal amount of hijiki or ½ cup (125 mL) wakame for the arame.

To finish this dish I like to toss it with 1 tbsp (15 mL) raw sesame seeds and 1 tbsp (15 mL) chopped green onion (green part only).

Creamed Garlic Spinach

Creamy, garlicky spinach is a classic flavor combination from my childhood. This healthier raw version retains all the nutritional content of the baby spinach while sacrificing none of the original dish's taste.

Makes 2 side servings

Tips

You may substitute 2 bunches roughly chopped field or bunched spinach for the baby spinach.

Cashews provide protein, copper, zinc, phosphorus, potassium and magnesium, as well as healthy monounsaturated fat.

Garlic cloves come in all sizes. If the cloves you are using are large, reduce the amount called for in this recipe to 2 cloves. If they are small, increase to 8 cloves. Remember, you can always add more but you can't take away, so be careful not to overdo it.

4 cups	packed baby spinach (see Tips, left)	1 L
2 tbsp	cold-pressed (extra virgin) olive oil	30 mL
3 tbsp	freshly squeezed lemon juice, divided	45 mL
1 tsp	fine sea salt, divided	5 mL
1 cup	whole raw cashews	250 mL
¾ cup	filtered water	175 mL
6	cloves garlic (see Tips, left)	6

1. In a bowl, combine spinach, olive oil, 1 tbsp (15 mL) lemon juice and ½ tsp (2 mL) salt. Toss until well combined. Cover and set aside for 10 minutes, until softened.

2. In a blender, combine cashews, water, garlic and remaining lemon juice and salt. Blend at high speed until smooth. Transfer 1 cup (250 mL) marinated spinach to blender. Blend at high speed until smooth.

3. Pour spinach-cashew purée over remaining marinated spinach and mix well. Serve immediately or cover and refrigerate for up to 2 days.

Green Beans Amandine

A healthy, delicious spin on a classic, this side dish is best served with main courses that are rich in flavor, such as Shepherd's Pie (page 166) or "Steak and Potatoes" (page 170).

**Makes
2 side servings**

Tips

Slice the green beans lengthwise on an angle to expose their soft flesh, which allows the marinade to penetrate and soften them. If lengthwise slicing proves too difficult, cut them in 1-inch (2.5 cm) pieces widthwise.

If you are lucky enough to own an electric food dehydrator, after Step 2, place the green beans on a nonstick dehydrator sheet and dehydrate at 105°F (41°C) for 30 minutes or until slightly softened.

½ cup	whole raw almonds	125 mL
1 tbsp	nutritional yeast	15 mL
1 tsp	fine sea salt, divided	5 mL
3 cups	sliced green beans (see Tips, left)	750 mL
3 tbsp	cold-pressed (extra virgin) olive oil	45 mL
2 tbsp	freshly squeezed lemon juice	30 mL

1. In a food processor fitted with the metal blade, combine almonds, nutritional yeast and ¼ tsp (1 mL) salt. Process until coarsely chopped (you want to retain some texture). Transfer to a bowl and set aside.

2. In a separate bowl, toss green beans with olive oil, lemon juice and remaining salt and mix well. Set aside for 10 minutes, until softened.

3. Add three-quarters of the almond mixture to the green beans and toss until well coated. Transfer to a serving bowl and garnish with remaining almond mixture. Serve immediately or cover and refrigerate for up to 3 days.

Almond Apple Holiday Stuffing

This stuffing will fool even the staunchest turkey-lover. Fresh celery, poultry seasoning and crisp apple help to make this an authentic-tasting holiday dish.

Makes 4 side servings

Tips

To soak the almonds, place in a bowl with 2 cups (500 mL) warm water. Cover and set aside for 10 minutes. Drain, discarding soaking liquid. Rinse under cold running water until the water runs clear.

Poultry seasoning is an aromatic blend of dried herbs and spices. The most common blend combines sage, thyme, marjoram, rosemary, nutmeg and black pepper. You may substitute 3 tbsp (45 mL) roughly chopped fresh sage leaves for the poultry seasoning.

1 cup	whole raw almonds, soaked (see Tips, left)	250 mL
$\frac{1}{2}$ cup	chopped apple	125 mL
$\frac{1}{2}$ cup	chopped celery	125 mL
$\frac{1}{4}$ cup	filtered water	60 mL
2 tsp	poultry seasoning (see Tips, left)	10 mL
1 tsp	fine sea salt	5 mL

1. In a food processor fitted with the metal blade, pulse soaked almonds, apple, celery, water, poultry seasoning and salt until roughly chopped (you want to retain some texture). Transfer to a bowl. Serve immediately or cover and refrigerate for up to 3 days.

Variation

Try adding $\frac{1}{4}$ cup (60 mL) grated carrot to this recipe.

Sunflower Seed "Refried Beans"

This dish is a blend of creamy sunflower seeds, aromatic cumin and slightly spicy chili powder. I love to serve it on a bed of crisp romaine topped with chunks of ripe avocado and drizzled with Mexican Fiesta Dressing (page 27).

Makes
1½ cups (375 mL)

Tips

To soak the sun-dried tomatoes, place ½ cup (125 mL) dry-packed sun-dried tomatoes in a bowl with 2 cups (500 mL) hot water. Cover and set aside for 10 minutes. Drain, discarding soaking water.

To soak the sunflower seeds, place in a bowl and cover with 3 cups (750 mL) hot water. Cover and set aside to soak for 10 minutes. Drain, discarding soaking water, and rinse under cold running water until the water runs clear.

½ cup	finely sliced soaked sun-dried tomatoes (see Tips, left)	125 mL
6 tbsp	filtered water	90 mL
3 tbsp	freshly squeezed lemon juice	45 mL
2 tbsp	chili powder	30 mL
1 tbsp	ground cumin	15 mL
1½ cups	raw sunflower seeds, soaked (see Tips, left)	375 mL

1. In a food processor fitted with the metal blade, combine soaked sun-dried tomatoes, water, lemon juice, chili powder and cumin. Process until smooth. Add soaked sunflower seeds and process until smooth, stopping motor to scrape down sides of work bowl as necessary. Transfer to a bowl. Serve immediately or cover and refrigerate for up to 5 days.

Variation

Curry Sunflower Seed Dip: Substitute an equal amount of mild curry powder for the chili powder and substitute 2 tbsp (30 mL) chopped peeled gingerroot for the tomatoes. Decrease the cumin to ½ tsp (2 mL).

Cheesy Broccoli

This dish uses nutritional yeast to create a cheesy sauce for broccoli without the use of dairy products. It's equally tasty made with kale, cauliflower or spinach.

Makes 2 side servings

Tips

To cut the broccoli into florets, use a sharp chef's knife to remove the large stem. Cut the florets into pieces approximately 1 inch (2.5 cm) in diameter.

Save broccoli stems for later use; they are very flavorful and contain a lot of nutrition. Use a vegetable peeler to peel the stem and expose the tender core, which is edible and can be served raw.

Nutritional yeast flakes can be found in well-stocked supermarkets and natural foods stores. Although not a raw product, nutritional yeast is fortified with vitamin B_{12} and helps to produce umami, the savory flavor sometimes lacking in vegetarian cuisine.

2 cups	broccoli florets (see Tips, left)	500 mL
1/4 cup	freshly squeezed lemon juice, divided	60 mL
1/2 tsp	fine sea salt, divided	2 mL
1/2 cup	whole raw cashews	125 mL
1/4 cup	nutritional yeast (see Tips, left)	60 mL
3 tbsp	filtered water	45 mL

1. In a bowl, combine broccoli, 2 tbsp (30 mL) lemon juice and a pinch of salt. Toss until well combined. Set aside for 10 minutes, until softened.
2. In a blender, combine cashews, nutritional yeast, water and remaining lemon juice and salt. Blend at high speed until smooth.
3. Add sauce to marinated broccoli and toss to coat evenly. Serve immediately or cover and refrigerate for up to 2 days.

Variations

Substitute 3 cups (750 mL) finely sliced kale or 4 cups (1 L) spinach for the broccoli.

Cheesy Shoestring Jicama Fries

The marinade for this recipe not only helps break down the texture of the jicama but also provides a rich, cheesy flavor.

Tips

Jicama tastes like a blend of apple, potato and celery. It is mildly sweet and has a high water content.

To trim the jicama, use a chef's knife to remove a small slice from all four sides to square it off before peeling.

If, like me, you prefer fatter "fries," after cutting the jicama into slices, cut it into strips approximately 1 inch (2.5 cm) wide.

• **Mandoline**

1	large jicama, peeled (see Tips, left)	1
½ cup	whole raw cashews	125 mL
½ cup	nutritional yeast	125 mL
¼ cup	filtered water	60 mL
¼ cup	cold-pressed (extra virgin) olive oil	60 mL
3 tbsp	freshly squeezed lemon juice	45 mL
½ tsp	fine sea salt	2 mL

1. Using mandoline, slice jicama lengthwise into pieces approximately ¼ inch (0.5 cm) thick. Stack the slices on top of each other and, using a sharp chef's knife, cut lengthwise into strips approximately ¼ inch (0.5 cm) wide. Cover and set aside.

2. In a blender, combine cashews, nutritional yeast, water, olive oil, lemon juice and salt. Blend at high speed until smooth.

3. In a bowl, toss jicama slices with sauce until well coated. Serve immediately or cover and refrigerate for up to 2 days.

Variation

Southwest Chili Cheese Fries: Add ½ cup (125 mL) Spiced Nut Crumble (page 30) and drizzle about ¼ cup (60 mL) Mexican Fiesta Dressing (page 27) overtop. Garnish with 2 to 3 tbsp (30 to 45 mL) chopped green onion (green part only).

Desserts

Desserts: rich, creamy, decadent — and nutritious — sweet treats. On a raw food diet you can enjoy dessert knowing that you are consuming healthful ingredients. Instead of using high-fat dairy products, a creamy texture is achieved with nuts, nut butters and coconut products. Soaked seeds such as flax seeds or even finely ground almonds and cashews take the place of refined flour and eggs. Other raw ingredients — cacao powder, coconut and hemp seeds — contain health-promoting ingredients such as phytonutrients, and they are simply delicious.

Instead of refined sugar, raw food desserts are sweetened with fresh fruit, dates or raw agave nectar, a sap that is extracted at low temperatures from the piña, or center, of the agave plant, which is native to Mexico. Other natural sweeteners that are making their way into the marketplace include raw coconut nectar, raw *lúcuma* powder and raw *yacón* syrup. The recipes in this book have been tested using raw agave nectar, but feel free to alter them by using your natural sweetener of choice.

The recipes in this chapter are particularly easy to make because they require no more than five ingredients, but that doesn't make them any less indulgent. Some of my favorites are White Chocolate and Coconut Cream (page 208), Coconut Macaroons (page 201) and Avocado Mint Pudding (page 190). Try them and you'll see that raw food desserts can be just as rich and sinfully delicious as their traditional counterparts. Because all the ingredients are fresh and unrefined, their luscious flavors shine through.

Watermelon Mint Refresher

Frozen watermelon and mint are a match made in heaven. When temperatures rise, grab your spoon and a bowl of this sweet, light, refreshing treat.

Makes 1 serving

Tips

When purchasing agave nectar, be sure to look for products labeled "raw." Most of the agave nectar on the market has been heated to a high temperature and does not qualify as raw food. If you have concerns, ask your purveyor.

Most flavoring extracts are not raw. Check the labels or contact purveyors if you have concerns. However, in raw food cuisine most organic extracts are acceptable, even those that have been distilled with steam.

2 cups	frozen cubed (2 inches/5 cm) watermelon	500 mL
3 tbsp	raw agave nectar (see Tips, left)	45 mL
1 tbsp	finely grated lemon zest	15 mL
1 tsp	raw mint extract (see Tips, left)	5 mL
¼ cup	roughly chopped fresh mint leaves	60 mL

1. In a food processor fitted with the metal blade, combine watermelon, agave nectar, lemon zest, mint extract and fresh mint. Pulse mixture 8 to 10 times or until roughly chopped. Transfer to a serving bowl and enjoy immediately.

Variation

Strawberry Mint Refresher: Substitute an equal amount of frozen chopped hulled strawberries for the watermelon.

Avocado Mint Pudding

This dessert is a creamy treat that uses the fat in soft avocado to create a rich pudding. Serve this with some fresh berries and a sprinkling of raw shelled hemp seeds.

Makes 4 or 5 servings

Tips

Use a soft, ripe avocado for this recipe. To ripen avocados, place them in a brown paper bag with a tomato or an apple. If your avocado is ripe and won't be consumed within a day or two, place it in the coolest part of the refrigerator to lengthen its life by three to four days. Once you take an avocado out of the fridge, do not put it back in, or it will turn black.

Most flavoring extracts are not raw. Check the labels or contact purveyors if you have concerns. However, in raw food cuisine most organic extracts are acceptable, even those that have been distilled with steam.

1	medium avocado (see Tips, left)	1
½ cup	raw agave nectar	125 mL
1 tsp	raw mint extract (see Tips, left)	5 mL
½ tsp	raw vanilla extract	2 mL
¼ cup	thinly sliced fresh mint leaves	60 mL

1. In a food processor fitted with the metal blade, combine avocado, agave nectar, mint extract and vanilla. Process until smooth, stopping motor to scrape down sides of work bowl as necessary. Transfer to a bowl.

2. Add fresh mint and mix until well combined. Serve immediately or cover and refrigerate for up to 2 days.

Variations

Chocolate Mint Avocado Pudding: Replace the fresh mint in Step 2 with ¼ cup (60 mL) raw cacao powder.

Lime Avocado Coconut Balls: Omit the mint extract and fresh mint. In Step 1, add ¼ cup (60 mL) freshly squeezed lime juice, ¼ cup (60 mL) melted coconut oil and 3 tbsp (45 mL) coconut butter. Transfer mixture to a shallow baking dish and freeze for 60 minutes. Using a tablespoon (15 mL), scoop up 15 to 20 portions and drop onto a baking sheet lined with parchment. Freeze for 15 minutes. Serve immediately or transfer to an airtight container and refrigerate for up to 5 days.

Spiced Banana Walnut Pudding

The combination of dates and bananas in this recipe adds a toffee flavor that is sure to satisfy any sweet tooth.

1½ cups	chopped banana	375 mL
½ cup	raw agave nectar	125 mL
½ cup	melted coconut oil (see Tips, left)	125 mL
2 tsp	ground cinnamon	10 mL
½ cup	raw walnut pieces or halves	125 mL

Makes 4 or 5 servings

Tips

Coconut oil is solid at room temperature but has a melting point of 76°F (24°C), so it is easy to liquefy. To melt it, place in a shallow glass bowl over a pot of simmering water.

Use high-quality organic cinnamon. You will get the freshest flavor by grinding whole cinnamon sticks in a spice grinder.

1. In a food processor fitted with the metal blade, combine banana, agave nectar, coconut oil and cinnamon. Process until smooth. Add walnuts and pulse 8 to 10 times or until roughly chopped. Transfer to a bowl. Serve immediately or cover and refrigerate for up to 3 days.

Variations

I like to add a dash of raw vanilla extract to this recipe.

Chocolate Walnut Toffee Pudding: Substitute 2 tbsp (30 mL) raw cacao powder for the ground cinnamon.

Cinnamon Peach Pudding

This pudding combines nutrient-dense peaches with rich coconut oil and healthy chia seeds. Make this in the summer when peaches are in season, juicy and ripe.

Makes 2 to 3 servings

Tips

To slice peaches, run a paring knife around the middle of the peach through to the stone. Using your hands, twist the fruit into two halves. Slice the half without the stone into the desired number of pieces. For the other half, use your knife to loosen and remove the stone before slicing.

When soaked, chia seeds can swell up to nine times their original size. This typically takes between 10 and 15 minutes, so be patient when working with them.

Two tablespoons (30 mL) chia seeds provides about 7 grams of alpha-linolenic acid (ALA), an omega-3 fat that is an essential fatty acid — without it, we could not survive. It is called "essential" because our bodies are unable to make it and we must obtain it from food. Good sources of ALA include flax seeds, chia seeds and walnuts.

2 cups	sliced peaches (see Tips, left)	500 mL
½ cup	chia seeds (see Tips, left)	125 mL
¼ cup	filtered water	60 mL
¼ cup	melted coconut oil	60 mL
3 tbsp	raw agave nectar	45 mL
1 tsp	ground cinnamon	5 mL

1. In a blender, combine peaches, chia seeds, water, coconut oil, agave nectar and cinnamon. Blend at high speed until smooth. Transfer to a bowl, cover and set aside for about 10 minutes to allow the chia seeds to absorb the liquid and swell. Serve immediately or cover and refrigerate for up to 2 days.

Summer Berry Parfait

This light, creamy treat is a mixture of fresh berries, sweet agave nectar and vanilla. I like to serve it to guests with a large dollop of Chocolate Fondue (page 32).

Makes 1 serving

Tips

To soak the cashews, place them in a bowl with 2 cups (500 mL) hot water. Cover and set aside for 10 minutes. Drain, discarding soaking water, and rinse under cold running water until the water runs clear.

You can substitute an equal amount of raspberries for the strawberries.

- Parfait glass

1 cup	whole raw cashews, soaked (see Tips, left)	250 mL
1 cup	chopped hulled strawberries, divided (see Tips, left)	250 mL
½ cup	filtered water	125 mL
¼ cup	raw agave nectar	60 mL
½ tsp	raw vanilla extract	2 mL
½ cup	blueberries	125 mL

1. In a blender, combine ½ cup (125 mL) strawberries, soaked cashews, water, agave nectar and vanilla. Blend at high speed until smooth.

2. Place a layer of strawberry cashew cream in parfait glass. Add a layer of blueberries, then another layer of cashew cream, followed by a layer of strawberries. Repeat 3 or 4 times until all the ingredients are used up. Serve immediately or cover and refrigerate for up to 2 days.

Dark Cherry Cream

Enjoy this rich, sweet cream on its own or with a mixture of fresh berries, raw walnuts and apple slices.

**Makes
1¼ cups (300 mL)**

Tips

To soak the cashews, place in a bowl with 1 cup (250 mL) warm water. Cover and set aside for 10 minutes. Drain, discarding soaking water, and rinse under cold running water until the water runs clear.

To remove the pit from a cherry, place it on a cutting board and gently push down on it with the butt end of a chef's knife to loosen the stone. Remove the pit with your fingers and discard.

If you are lucky enough to have a high-powered blender, use it for this recipe.

½ cup	whole raw cashews, soaked (see Tips, left)	125 mL
1 cup	pitted dark cherries (see Tips, left)	250 mL
¼ cup	filtered water	60 mL
¼ cup	raw agave nectar	60 mL
½ tsp	raw vanilla extract	2 mL

1. In a blender, combine cherries, soaked cashews, water, agave nectar and vanilla. Blend at high speed until smooth. Serve immediately or cover and refrigerate for up to 5 days.

Variations

Mixed Berry Cream: Substitute ¼ cup (60 mL) blueberries, ¼ cup (60 mL) raspberries and ¾ cup (175 mL) chopped hulled strawberries for the cherries.

Dark Cherry Chocolate Cream: Add 2 tbsp (30 mL) raw cacao powder.

Chunky Banana Cacao Soft-Serve

This delicious "soft-serve" is sure to trick any ice cream–lover into thinking it contains dairy. The simplicity of this recipe, combined with its rich, creamy banana flavor and cacao crunch, will make this one of your go-to treats.

Makes 2 servings

Tips

To prepare the bananas for this recipe, peel and cut them into 2-inch (5 cm) chunks. Place in an airtight container and freeze for up to 1 hour (for small to medium-sized bananas) or up to $1\frac{1}{2}$ hours (for large bananas), until frozen.

If you prefer a sweeter ice cream, add the agave nectar.

Try adding your favorite fresh fruit, such as papaya, peaches, pears, plums or mango, to the soft-serve. Cut into 1-inch (2.5 cm) cubes and add just before serving or prior to freezing.

4	large bananas, cut into chunks and frozen (see Tips, left)	4
2 tbsp	raw cacao nibs	30 mL
1 tsp	raw vanilla extract	5 mL
2 tbsp	raw agave nectar, optional (see Tips, left)	30 mL
$\frac{1}{4}$ to $\frac{1}{2}$ cup	Nut Milk (page 19)	60 to 125 mL

1. In a food processor fitted with the metal blade, combine bananas, cacao nibs, vanilla and agave nectar (if using). Process until chopped. With machine running, drizzle in nut milk through the feed tube, $\frac{1}{4}$ cup (60 mL) at a time, until mixture becomes smooth. Divide between two serving bowls. Serve immediately or transfer to an airtight container and freeze for up to 3 days.

Variation

Chocolate Banana Soft-Serve: Substitute $\frac{1}{4}$ cup (60 mL) raw cacao powder for the cacao nibs and increase the agave nectar to $\frac{1}{4}$ cup (60 mL).

Banana Split

Pure, rich, dark chocolate sauce, juicy berries and luscious ripe banana — who doesn't love a banana split? Relive your childhood with this decadent treat. For an extra-special dessert, serve it with a dollop of Lemon Vanilla Cashew Yogurt (page 47).

Makes 1 serving

Tip

When purchasing agave nectar, be sure to look for products labeled "raw." Most of the agave nectar on the market has been heated to a high temperature and does not qualify as raw food. If you have concerns, ask your purveyor.

½ cup	chopped hulled strawberries	125 mL
2 tbsp	raw agave nectar (see Tip, left)	30 mL
1 tbsp	freshly squeezed lemon juice	15 mL
1	banana, sliced in half lengthwise	1
¼ cup	Chocolate Fondue (page 32)	60 mL

1. In a bowl, combine strawberries, agave nectar and lemon juice. Cover and set aside for 10 minutes, until softened.
2. Lay banana halves flat on a serving plate. Top with strawberries and chocolate fondue. Enjoy immediately.

Variations

Try substituting an equal amount of blueberries or raspberries for the strawberries.

I like to add a dash of raw vanilla extract to the strawberries in Step 1 and to sprinkle 1 tsp (5 mL) raw cacao nibs over the finished dessert.

Pistachio Halva Balls

This traditional European recipe is a delight in both flavor and texture. I love the creaminess of the sesame paste paired with crunchy sesame seeds and pistachios.

Makes 15 balls

Tips

When purchasing nuts, be sure to look for products labeled "raw." Most of the nuts on the market have been roasted and do not qualify as raw food. If you have concerns, ask your purveyor.

Tahini is a paste or butter made from ground sesame seeds that is similar to peanut or almond butter. Most store-bought tahini is made from sesame seeds that have been roasted, depriving it of its raw status. If you are following a strictly raw diet, be sure to look for products labeled "raw."

When handling the pistachio balls, moisten your hands with water to prevent the mixture from sticking to your fingers.

- **Baking sheet lined with parchment**

½ cup	whole raw pistachios (see Tips, left)	125 mL
1 cup	raw sesame seeds, divided	250 mL
¼ cup	raw tahini (see Tips, left)	60 mL
¼ cup	raw agave nectar	60 mL
1 tsp	raw vanilla extract	5 mL

1. In a food processor fitted with the metal blade, process pistachios until roughly chopped (you want to retain some texture). Transfer to a bowl.
2. Using same work bowl, add ¾ cup (175 mL) sesame seeds, tahini, agave nectar and vanilla. Process until well combined. Transfer to a bowl.
3. Add chopped pistachios to sesame-tahini mixture and mix until well combined. Using a tablespoon (15 mL), scoop up 15 equal portions. Roll each between the palms of your hands to make a ball (see Tips, left). Spread remaining sesame seeds on a piece of parchment and roll balls in seeds, coating them evenly. Place on prepared baking sheet. Freeze for 10 minutes or until firm. Serve immediately or transfer to an airtight container and refrigerate for up to 7 days.

Variation

Substitute 1 cup (250 mL) whole raw cashews for the pistachios.

Almond Bliss Balls

These sinfully rich treats are sure to fool even the biggest dessert fan into thinking they are bad for you. I like serving them during the holiday season at family gatherings.

Makes 15 balls	

Tips

Almonds are very nutritious. They include phytochemicals, protein, fiber and healthy fats, as well as vitamin E, magnesium, phosphorus, potassium, manganese and a small amount of B vitamins.

When handling the almond balls, moisten your hands with water to prevent the mixture from sticking to your fingers.

The balls can be kept in the freezer in an airtight container for up to two months.

- **Baking sheet lined with parchment**

½ cup	whole raw almonds	125 mL
½ cup	raw almond butter	125 mL
¼ cup	raw agave nectar	60 mL
3 tbsp	melted coconut oil	45 mL
2 tbsp	coconut butter	30 mL

1. In a food processor fitted with the metal blade, process almonds until roughly chopped. Set aside.

2. In a mixing bowl, combine almond butter, agave nectar, coconut oil and coconut butter. Mix well. Using a tablespoon (15 mL), scoop up 15 equal portions. Roll each between your hands to make a ball (see Tips, left). Spread chopped almonds on a piece of parchment and roll balls in nuts, coating evenly. Place on prepared baking sheet. Freeze for 10 minutes or until firm. Serve immediately or transfer to an airtight container and refrigerate for up to 7 days (see Tips, left).

Variation

I like to add a pinch of ground cinnamon in Step 2.

Chocolate Coconut Bark

Reminiscent of crispy milk chocolate treats, this bark is crunchy and creamy, with a rich, dark chocolate finish — and a lot healthier for you!

Makes 10 to 12 small servings

Tips

Coconut oil is solid at room temperature but has a melting point of 76°F (24°C), so it is easy to liquefy. To melt it, place in a shallow glass bowl over a pot of simmering water.

Cacao powder is powdered raw chocolate. It is similar to cocoa powder but tastes even better, with a deeper, richer flavor. Cacao powder is available in well-stocked supermarkets, natural foods stores and online. If you are transitioning to a raw food diet and can't find it, you may substitute an equal quantity of good-quality cocoa powder, but note that the beans in cocoa powder have been roasted, depriving them of their raw status. If you are following a strictly raw diet, use cacao powder.

- Baking sheet lined with parchment

½ cup	melted coconut oil (see Tips, left)	125 mL
¼ cup	coconut butter	60 mL
¼ cup	raw agave nectar	60 mL
¼ cup	raw cacao powder (see Tips, left)	60 mL
1½ cups	dried shredded coconut	375 mL

1. In a food processor fitted with the metal blade, process coconut oil, coconut butter, agave nectar and cacao powder until smooth. Add shredded coconut and pulse 6 to 8 times or until combined.

2. Using a rubber spatula, spread mixture on prepared baking sheet in a thin layer approximately ¼ inch (0.5 cm) thick. Freeze for 10 to 12 minutes or until set. Break into 10 to 12 pieces. Serve immediately or transfer to an airtight container and refrigerate for up to 7 days.

Variations

For more protein, add ¼ cup (60 mL) raw shelled hemp seeds or 2 tbsp (30 mL) raw pumpkin seeds. You can also add various combinations of raw nuts such as walnuts or cashews.

For an even more decadent treat, dip the bark in Chocolate Fondue (page 32) or Lemon Vanilla Cashew Yogurt (page 47) after it has been broken into pieces.

Lemon Vanilla Coconut Bark: Substitute 2 tbsp (30 mL) lemon zest for the cacao powder and add 1 tsp (5 mL) raw vanilla extract.

Pecan Pie Brownies

Dense pecans, aromatic cinnamon and sweet dates make these a satisfying treat. Dip them in Chocolate Fondue (page 32) and enjoy with a tall glass of Nut Milk (page 19).

Makes 6 brownies

Tips

Be careful not to overprocess the pecans. You want the nuts to be broken down but not so processed that they become nut butter.

If the dates you are using are not soft, soak them in 1 cup (250 mL) warm water for 10 minutes and then drain, discarding the soaking liquid.

When shopping for dates, always look for the Medjool variety. They are larger, softer and, in my opinion, the most flavorful. Dates provide iron, fiber and potassium and are also a good source of antioxidants.

Although dates are a healthy whole food, they are high in sugar. When you find yourself craving refined sugar, reach for one or two dates and you will find the craving goes away.

- **4-inch (10 cm) square glass baking dish**

1 cup	whole raw pecans	250 mL
2 tsp	ground cinnamon	10 mL
1 tsp	raw cacao powder	5 mL
5	chopped pitted dates (see Tips, left)	5
2 tbsp	raw agave nectar	30 mL

1. In a food processor fitted with the metal blade, combine pecans, cinnamon and cacao powder. Process until coarsely chopped (see Tips, left). Add dates and process until mixture is combined and no large pieces remain. Add agave nectar and pulse 5 or 6 times to combine.
2. Transfer to baking dish and spread evenly. Refrigerate for about 12 minutes, or until slightly firm. Cut into 6 equal pieces. Serve immediately or cover and refrigerate for up to 3 days.

Coconut Macaroons

I love the sweet, rich flavor of the coconut and vanilla combination in this recipe. As an added treat, I enjoy dipping these in a little Chocolate Fondue (page 32).

**Makes
15 macaroons**

Tips

Coconut butter is a blend of coconut oil and coconut meat. You can usually find it in natural foods stores next to the coconut oil.

Coconut oil is solid at room temperature but has a melting point of 76°F (24°C), so it is easy to liquefy. To melt it, place in a shallow glass bowl over a pot of simmering water.

Most flavoring extracts are not raw. Check the labels or contact purveyors if you have concerns. However, in raw food cuisine most organic extracts are acceptable, even those that have been distilled with steam.

Use unsweetened medium-shred unsulfured coconut. Not only is this type of coconut nutritionally beneficial, the medium shred size will help the macaroons hold together.

- **Baking sheet lined with parchment**

¼ cup	coconut butter (see Tips, left)	60 mL
¼ cup	raw agave nectar	60 mL
3 tbsp	melted coconut oil (see Tips, left)	45 mL
1 tsp	raw vanilla extract (see Tips, left)	5 mL
2 cups	dried shredded coconut (see Tips, left)	500 mL

1. In a food processor fitted with the metal blade, process coconut butter, agave nectar, coconut oil and vanilla until smooth. Add shredded coconut and pulse 8 to 10 times to combine. Transfer to a bowl.

2. Using a tablespoon (15 mL), scoop up 15 equal portions and drop on prepared baking sheet. Freeze for 10 minutes or until firm. Serve immediately or transfer to an airtight container and refrigerate for up to 7 days.

Hazelnut Cacao Macaroons

The rich flavors of chocolate and hazelnut combined with sweet coconut make this a dessert that can be enjoyed any time of the year. I enjoy eating these with a tall glass of Nut Milk (page 19).

**Makes
15 macaroons**

Tips

Cacao powder is powdered raw chocolate. It is similar to cocoa powder but tastes even better, with a deeper, richer flavor. Cacao powder is available in well-stocked supermarkets, natural foods stores and online. If you are transitioning to a raw food diet and can't find it, you may substitute an equal quantity of good-quality cocoa powder, but note that the beans in cocoa powder have been roasted, depriving them of their raw status. If you are following a strictly raw diet, use cacao powder.

Use unsweetened medium-shred unsulfured coconut. Not only is this type of coconut nutritionally beneficial, the medium shred size will help hold the macaroons together.

You can use a small ice-cream scoop to portion these out.

½ cup	whole raw hazelnuts	125 mL
¼ cup	raw cacao powder (see Tips, left)	60 mL
¼ cup	raw agave nectar	60 mL
3 tbsp	melted coconut oil	45 mL
Pinch	fine sea salt	Pinch
½ cup	dried shredded coconut (see Tips, left)	125 mL

1. In a food processor fitted with the metal blade, process hazelnuts and cacao powder until roughly chopped (you want to retain some texture). Add agave nectar, coconut oil and salt; pulse 5 to 6 times to combine. Add shredded coconut and pulse 8 to 10 times to combine. Transfer to a bowl.

2. Using a tablespoon (15 mL), scoop up 15 equal portions and drop on prepared baking sheet (see Tips, left). Freeze for 10 minutes or until firm. Serve immediately or transfer to an airtight container and refrigerate for up to 7 days.

Strawberry Coconut Shortcake Tart

This luscious dessert is a creamy mixture of rich coconut butter, juicy strawberries, aromatic vanilla and sweet agave nectar — perfect for serving at special parties.

Makes 2 servings

Tips

You may need to add a bit more water in Step 1, depending on the texture of the coconut butter. If the mixture is too thick, add 1 tbsp (15 mL) water at a time as needed.

Coconut butter is a blend of coconut oil and coconut meat. You can usually find it in natural foods stores next to the coconut oil.

Try substituting an equal quantity of cashews for the almonds.

• **Two 4-inch (10 cm) quiche molds, lined with plastic wrap**

1 cup	chopped hulled strawberries, divided	250 mL
½ cup	coconut butter (see Tips, left)	125 mL
6 tbsp	raw agave nectar, divided	90 mL
3 tbsp	filtered water	45 mL
1 tsp	raw vanilla extract	5 mL
1 cup	whole raw almonds (see Tips, left)	250 mL

1. In a blender, combine ¾ cup (175 mL) strawberries, coconut butter, ¼ cup (60 mL) agave nectar, water and vanilla. Blend at high speed until smooth, stopping machine to scrape down sides of jar as necessary (see Tips, left).

2. In a food processor fitted with the metal blade, process almonds until flour-like in consistency. With the motor running, drizzle in remaining agave nectar. Pulse to combine.

3. Divide mixture in half and press into prepared quiche molds. Top with strawberry-coconut purée, dividing equally. Top with remaining strawberries, dividing equally. Serve immediately or cover and refrigerate for up to 3 days.

Pineapple Coconut Crumble

This sweet, crumbly treat is a blend of juicy pineapple and rich coconut oil topped with a crisp almond and coconut crust.

Makes 4 or 5 servings

Tips

When shopping for dates, always look for the Medjool variety. They are larger, softer and, in my opinion, the most flavorful. Dates provide iron, fiber and potassium and are also a good source of antioxidants.

Although dates are a healthy whole food, they are high in sugar. When you find yourself craving refined sugar, reach for one or two dates and you will find the craving goes away.

Coconut oil is solid at room temperature but has a melting temperature of 76°F (24°C), so it is easy to liquefy. To melt it, place in a shallow glass bowl over a pot of simmering water.

Use unsweetened medium-shred unsulfured coconut. Not only is this type of coconut nutritionally beneficial, the medium shred size will help the crust hold together.

- **4-inch (10 cm) square glass baking dish**

2 cups	pineapple cut in 1-inch (2.5 cm) pieces, divided	500 mL
¼ cup	filtered water	60 mL
9	chopped pitted dates, divided	9
3 tbsp	melted coconut oil (see Tips, left)	45 mL
1½ cups	whole raw almonds	375 mL
½ cup	dried shredded coconut (see Tips, left)	125 mL
Pinch	fine sea salt	Pinch

1. In a blender, combine 1 cup (250 mL) pineapple, water, a third of the dates and the coconut oil. Blend at high speed until smooth. Fold in remaining pineapple. Transfer to baking dish and spread over bottom of dish.

2. In a food processor fitted with the metal blade, process almonds, shredded coconut and salt until just combined (you want to retain some texture). Add remaining dates and pulse until combined.

3. Spread almond mixture on top of pineapple mixture. Refrigerate for 10 minutes or until set. Serve immediately or cover and refrigerate for up to 3 days.

Mini Chocolate Banana Flax Cakes

These cakes are soft and dense and have a wonderful rich, dark chocolate flavor, with none of the hidden ingredients or unhealthy fats of traditional desserts. I like to serve them with a dollop of Chocolate Fondue (page 32) and some Lemon Vanilla Cashew Yogurt (page 47).

Makes 6 small cakes

Tips

When purchasing agave nectar, be sure to look for products labeled "raw." Most of the agave nectar on the market has been heated to a high temperature and does not qualify as raw food. If you have concerns, ask your purveyor.

You can purchase flax seeds that are already ground (often described as "milled") in vacuum-sealed bags, or you can grind them yourself. To grind the flax for this recipe, place 1 cup (250 mL) whole flax seeds in a blender and process at high speed until finely ground.

- One $\frac{1}{2}$-cup (125 mL) ramekin, lined with plastic wrap

1½ cups	chopped bananas	375 mL
½ cup	raw agave nectar (see Tips, left)	125 mL
⅔ cup	raw cacao powder	150 mL
Dash	raw vanilla extract	Dash
1¾ cups	ground flax seeds (see Tips, left)	425 mL

1. In a food processor fitted with the metal blade, combine bananas, agave nectar, cacao powder and vanilla. Process until smooth, stopping motor to scrape down sides of work bowl as necessary. Transfer to a bowl.

2. Add ground flax seeds and mix well. Cover and set aside for 10 minutes to allow seeds to absorb the liquid and swell.

3. Using a ½-cup (125 mL) measure, scoop mixture into prepared ramekin and, using your fingers, gently press to distribute evenly. Turn ramekin over onto a serving plate and tap on the bottom to release cake. Repeat until all of the mixture has been used. Serve immediately or cover and refrigerate for up to 3 days.

Variation

Banana Cinnamon Flax Cakes: Substitute 1 tbsp (15 mL) ground cinnamon for the cacao powder and increase the vanilla extract to 2 tsp (10 mL).

Carrot Cake

This cake is sure to be a crowd-pleaser no matter where you go. I love the blend of sweet carrots, rich coconut and fragrant cinnamon.

Makes 2 to 3 servings

Tips

To soak the raisins, place in a bowl with ½ cup (125 mL) hot water. Cover and set aside for 10 minutes. Drain, discarding soaking liquid.

To remove excess water from shredded carrots, place them in a piece of cheesecloth and, using your hands, squeeze out the moisture. You can also use a nut-milk bag if you have one, or you can place the carrots in a fine-mesh sieve and use the back of a ladle to press out the excess water.

- **4-inch (10 cm) square glass baking dish**

1 cup	raw walnut halves	250 mL
¾ cup	chopped pitted dates	175 mL
¼ cup	raisins, soaked (see Tips, left)	60 mL
1 tsp	ground cinnamon	5 mL
3 cups	grated carrots, excess water removed (see Tips, left)	750 mL

1. In a food processor fitted with the metal blade, process walnuts, dates, soaked raisins and cinnamon until coarsely chopped (you want to retain some texture). Add shredded carrots and pulse to combine, about 8 to 10 times.

2. Transfer to baking dish and press down firmly, especially at the edges. Refrigerate for about 10 minutes or until firm throughout. Cut into 4 equal portions. Serve immediately or cover and refrigerate for up to 3 days.

Variations

I like to add a pinch of ground nutmeg and 3 tbsp (45 mL) dried shredded coconut in Step 1.

Frosted Carrot Cake: Multiply the ingredients by four and press into a 10-inch (25 cm) springform pan. Frost with a double batch of Lemon Vanilla Cashew Yogurt (page 47).

Raspberry Ganache

I love the rich blend of sweet raspberries and creamy coconut butter in this ganache. Serve it with a dollop of Berry Jam (page 31) and Lemon Vanilla Cashew Yogurt (page 47) alongside for a decadent dessert.

**Makes
2 cups (500 mL)**

Tips

When purchasing agave nectar, be sure to look for products labeled "raw." Most of the agave nectar on the market has been heated to a high temperature and does not qualify as raw food. If you have concerns, ask your purveyor.

Coconut butter is a blend of coconut oil and coconut meat. It is usually available in natural foods stores next to the coconut oil.

If you do not have access to coconut butter, increase the coconut oil to 1/2 cup (125 mL) and decrease the water to 2 tbsp (30 mL). Place the coconut oil in the refrigerator for 15 minutes to thicken before adding to the blender.

1 cup	fresh raspberries	250 mL
1/3 cup	raw agave nectar (see Tips, left)	75 mL
1/4 cup	warm filtered water	60 mL
1/4 cup	melted coconut oil	60 mL
1/4 cup	coconut butter (see Tips, left)	60 mL
1 tsp	raw vanilla extract	5 mL

1. In a blender, combine raspberries, agave nectar, water, coconut oil, coconut butter and vanilla. Blend at high speed until smooth. Transfer to a bowl. Cover and refrigerate for about 10 minutes, until slightly thickened. Serve immediately or cover and refrigerate for up to 3 days.

Variations

After blending, I like to stir in 1/4 cup (60 mL) fresh berries such as raspberries or blueberries.

Chocolate Raspberry Ganache: Add 3 tbsp (45 mL) raw cacao powder.

White Chocolate and Coconut Cream

This recipe for raw vegan white chocolate cream tastes like the most decadent dairy-based white chocolate. Eat it with a spoon right out of the blender or enjoy it drizzled over fresh strawberries.

....

Makes 1 cup

Tips

Cacao butter is solid at room temperature. With a melting point of 93°F (34°C), it is easy to liquefy. Simply place in a shallow glass bowl over a pot of simmering water.

To make the cashew flour, process cashews in a food processor fitted with the metal blade, until flour-like in consistency. Be careful not to overprocess — you want the nuts to be broken down and floury, not so processed that they become nut butter.

Coconut oil is solid at room temperature but has a melting temperature of 76°F (24°C), so it is easy to liquefy. To melt it, place in a shallow glass bowl over a pot of simmering water.

½ cup	melted cacao butter (see Tips, left)	125 mL
½ cup	raw cashew flour (see Tips, left)	125 mL
¼ cup	raw agave nectar	60 mL
3 tbsp	melted coconut oil (see Tips, left)	45 mL
1 tsp	raw vanilla extract	5 mL

1. In a blender, combine cacao butter, cashew flour, agave nectar, coconut oil and vanilla. Blend at high speed until smooth. Serve immediately.

Variation

Raw White Chocolate Squares: Prepare recipe as indicated. Pour mixture into a nonstick ice-cube tray and freeze for 1 hour or until firm enough to handle. Remove from freezer and allow to sit for 10 minutes to thaw slightly, to make it easier to release cubes from tray. Serve immediately or transfer to an airtight container and refrigerate for up to 5 days.

Buying Raw Ingredients

Because it is often difficult to recognize food products that qualify as raw, to help you through the transitioning process I have noted a few brands that pass muster. With the passage of time others will no doubt appear in the marketplace. As you become more comfortable with purchasing raw food products, you will be able to identify them yourself. If you have trouble locating some of the products, I have also included the names of several websites where you can order online. As people become more aware of raw foods, I'm confident that more and more of these products will become stock items at grocery stores.

Raw agave nectar
Agave nectar can be found on the shelves of most well-stocked supermarkets and in all natural foods stores. When purchasing agave nectar, make sure the label identifies it as raw and/or that it has been processed at acceptable temperatures. Brands to look for include Wholesome Sweeteners, Madhava Natural Sweeteners (raw grade) and Xagave.

Brown rice miso
Brown rice miso is made from whole fermented brown rice grains. Although not a raw food, it is commonly used in raw cuisine because it is gluten-free, mineral-rich and great for the digestion. You can find brown rice miso at well-stocked supermarkets and natural foods stores. Brands to look for include Eden Foods, Tradition and South River.

Raw cacao powder
Raw cacao can be found in natural foods stores and some well-stocked supermarkets. Brands to look for include Navitas Naturals and Organic Traditions.

Nut and seed butters
Most well-stocked grocery stores carry raw nut and/or seed butters. You will certainly be able to find them in natural foods stores. Check before purchasing to make sure that they are labeled "raw." Brands to look for include Artisana and Nuts to You nut butters.

Nutritional yeast
Nutritional yeast flakes can be found in well-stocked supermarkets and natural foods stores. Although not a raw product, nutritional yeast is fortified with vitamin B_{12}. When purchasing nutritional yeast, make sure it has been fortified. My favorite brands include Red Star, KAL and Lynside.

Olives
Raw olives are bitter and cannot be consumed; they must be cured. During the curing process most olives are heated or pasteurized, which deprives them of their raw status. Although not a raw product, olives cured in brine are often accepted in raw food diets because they are high in healthy fats. Look for bojita olives in an organic brine; they can be found in natural foods stores or through specialty health food retailers.

Protein powder
Raw protein powders can be found in natural foods stores and some well-stocked supermarkets. When purchasing protein powders, look for ones that have been sprouted and/or are labeled "raw." Some of my favorite brands include Manitoba Harvest, Sunwarrior, Garden of Life, Forever Healthy, Navitas Naturals, Ruth's Hemp Foods and Naturally Splendid.

Sea vegetables

Sea vegetables (seaweed) can be found in most well-stocked supermarkets and natural foods stores. Some are roasted before being packaged, so make sure to check the label to see if this is the case; generally they will not be labeled "raw." It is best to become familiar with brands that are raw, which include Eden Foods and Maine Coast Sea Vegetables.

Vanilla extract

You can find raw vanilla extract in most natural foods stores or at online specialty suppliers. Some well-stocked grocery stores also carry the product. Brands to look for include Nielsen-Massey, Lochhead, Arizona Vanilla Company and Vanillabazaar.

Wheat-free tamari

Wheat-free tamari can be found in natural foods stores and well-stocked supermarkets. Although not a raw product, wheat-free tamari is gluten-free. My favorite brands include San-J, Amano and Eden Foods.

Online Sources for Certified Raw Food Products

The following are leading websites for raw food products. I have included their geographic location to assist you when ordering.

- **Blue Mountain Organics**
  (Floyd, Virginia)
  www.bluemountainorganics.com

- **The Fresh Network**
  (Norwich, United Kingdom)
  www.fresh-network.com

- **Giddy YOYO**
  (Orangeville, Ontario)
  www.giddyyoyo.com

- **Raw Pleasure**
  (Queensland, Australia)
  http://raw-pleasure.com.au

- **Raw Power Australia**
  (Queensland, Australia)
  www.rawpower.com.au

- **Real Raw Food**
  (Vancouver, British Columbia)
  www.realrawfood.com

- **Raw Utopia**
  (Denver, Colorado)
  www.rawutopia.com

- **Sunfood Superfoods**
  (San Diego, California)
  www.sunfood.com

- **Truly Organic Foods**
  (Toronto, Ontario)
  www.trulyorganicfoods.com

- **Upaya Naturals**
  (Toronto, Ontario)
  www.upayanaturals.com

Index

Library and Archives Canada Cataloguing in Publication

McNish, Douglas, author
  Raw, quick & delicious! : 5-ingredient recipes in just 15 minutes / Douglas McNish.

Includes index.
ISBN 978-0-7788-0455-0 (pbk.)

1. Raw foods. 2. Raw food diet. 3. Quick and easy cooking. 4. Cookbooks.
I. Title. II. Title: Raw, quick and delicious!.

TX837.M293 2013   641.5'636   C2013-903351-3

More Great Books
from Robert Rose

Classic Bestsellers

- The Healing Herbs Cookbook
  by Pat Crocker
- The Juicing Bible, Second Edition
  by Pat Crocker
- The Smoothies Bible, Second Edition
  by Pat Crocker
- The Complete Whole Grains Cookbook
  by Judith Finlayson
- The Healthy Slow Cooker
  by Judith Finlayson
- 5 Easy Steps to Healthy Cooking
  by Camilla V. Saulsbury
- 500 Best Quinoa Recipes
  by Camilla V. Saulsbury
- The Leafy Greens Cookbook
  by Susan Sampson

Vegetarian and Vegan Cooking

- The Vegetarian Kitchen Table Cookbook
  by Igor Brotto and Olivier Guiriec
- The Vegetarian Cook's Bible
  by Pat Crocker
- The Vegan Cook's Bible
  by Pat Crocker
- The Vegetarian Slow Cooker
  by Judith Finlayson

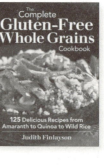

- Eat Raw, Eat Well
  by Douglas McNish
- The Best 30-Minute Vegetarian Recipes
  by Marie-Claude Morin
- 350 Best Vegan Recipes
  by Deb Roussou
- 150 Best Vegan Muffin Recipes
  by Camilla V. Saulsbury

Gluten-Free Cooking

- Complete Gluten-Free Diet & Nutrition Guide
  by Alexandra Anca and Theresa Santandrea-Cull
- The Complete Gluten-Free Whole Grains Cookbook
  by Judith Finlayson
- 150 Best Gluten-Free Muffin Recipes
  by Camilla V. Saulsbury
- 125 Best Gluten-Free Bread Machine Recipes
  by Donna Washburn and Heather Butt
- 250 Gluten-Free Favorites
  by Donna Washburn and Heather Butt
- Complete Gluten-Free Cookbook
  by Donna Washburn and Heather Butt
- Easy Everyday Gluten-Free Cooking
  by Donna Washburn and Heather Butt